I0528990

CLARITY
CONCEPTS

The Path for POSITIVE LIVING

JANE MARIE DOWNEY, M. ED

Published by
Hybrid Global Publishing
333 E 14th Street
#3C
New York, NY 10003

Copyright © 2024 by Jane Marie Downey, M. Ed

All rights reserved. No part of this book may be reproduced or transmitted in any form or by any means, electronic or mechanical, including photocopying, recording, or by any information storage and retrieval system, without the written permission of the Publisher, except where permitted by law.

Manufactured in the United States of America, or in the United Kingdom when distributed elsewhere.

Downey, M. Ed, Jane Marie.
Clarity Concepts
    ISBN: 978-1-961757-25-7
    eBook: 978-1-961757-26-4
    LCCN: 2023922758

Cover design by: Julia Kuris
Developmental Editor: Claudia Volkman
Copyediting by: Maureen Hoyt
Interior design by: Suba Murugan
Illustrations by: Dana Breslin, DB Creative
Author photo by: Ann Marie Casey

Back cover over Photograph by Lisa Eckl, Esq.
Messages in the Water by Masaru Emoto, (C) Office Masaru Emoto, LLC.
All Synonyms and Antonyms from Microsoft Word Thesaurus
Closing Session Mantra from Jackie Carroll, Personal Trainer
Career Advice from Leadership Professor Elaine Mercier
Morning Mantra from Mary O'Leary Dronson
All other book images were created and are owned by the author.
Clarity Concepts model graphic, DM Breslin Designs
Clarity Concepts Logo, DM Breslin Designs

www.ClarityConceptsInc.com

To my son, Mackie, the brightest light on Planet Earth
To Fiona Lally Ogilvie who encouraged me to start my own business and
helped me conceive the name Clarity Concepts™
To my sister Elizabeth Downey Miller for all of her love and support

CONTENTS

INTRODUCTION

Welcome to Clarity Concepts™ The Path for Positive Living! You may be wondering why you would want to read this book or take my advice. I am a successful business owner grounded in corporate insurance and accounting skills. During my career, I studied esoteric healing modalities, including Reiki, Touch for Health, Therapeutic Touch, the Labyrinth, Aromatherapy, Meditation, Yoga, Counseling, Psychology, Pilates, and other means of healing. I am certified in Holistic Health from Rosemont College, and I have a Master's Degree in Psychoeducational Processes (Group Dynamics) from Temple University. I also obtained a Certificate in Spiritual Psychology with Dr. Tom Legere, formerly of the Psychosynthesis Institute. I immersed myself for one unforgettable one-week intensive in Expressive Arts therapy with The California Institute for Integral Studies.

My work with the labyrinth led me to facilitate weeklong workshops at the Asilomar Conference Center on the Monterey Peninsula in California for The Centers for Spiritual Living. It was exhilarating to complete these studies when the concepts were new and foreign to many.

What really spoke to me were the teachings of Ernest Holmes from his *Science of Mind* spiritual principles, now rebranded as Centers for Spiritual Living (CSL). Holmes carefully studied the religions of the world, and his premise was **our thoughts create our reality**. Dr. Holmes' book, *Creative Mind and Success*[1], written in 1919 is a definitive example ot this premise.

1, Ernest Holmes, *Creative Mind and Success*, (New York, NY, McBride & Company, 1919, New York, NY, republished, Mansfield Center, CT, Martino Publishing, 2013)

He taught Affirmative Prayer as a way of working with Universal Power to craft the outcomes we are seeking. The buzzwords these days for creating such outcomes are **manifestation** or **demonstration.** This teaching is also known as *New Thought* because it changes the way we think about our relationship with Spirit and the Universe. As the Clarity Concepts ™ model shows, **our *actions* also create our reality**.

So, what is it you are seeking to manifest and what stands in the way of creating your desires? What is in your current thinking that is creating today's outcomes?

The Clarity Concepts ™ Model came to me in a meditation over 26 years ago just after I took a leap of faith and started my own consulting practice with only one four-month contract. Because I employed the CC Model since the beginning of my own business, I am happy to report I have been independent all these years. My work has been so successful, I found it hard to find time to write this book!

Twice I asked myself why the book was not complete. The first answer was that I needed to put my stories on paper showing my demonstrations. I couldn't just tell you what the steps of the model require; I needed to give you examples from my experience. Also, research on mindfulness, intention and spirituality has changed dramatically in recent years. In the reference section at the end of the book, I share with you links on the latest research about Happiness, Forgiveness, Affirmations, Gratitude, Meditation, Mindfulness, and Goal Setting, which have all been scientifically proven. The Clarity Concepts™ Model is no longer a conceptual approach; it is now grounded in significant research, providing assurance that it will guide you on your movement forward toward daily success.

The CC Model not only incorporates Holmes' work but also adds many facets from other spiritual and holistic modalities and scientific research to help you know and understand your power to create and achieve your desires. The *Clarity Concepts*™ Model shows you how to strengthen this one simple philosophy:

You attract what you think and with what you resonate.

Well-known channeler Esther Hicks (Abraham) named it the *Law of Attraction.*[2] She says, *The Law of Attraction and its magnetic power reaches out into the Universe and attracts other thoughts that are vibrationally like it.* Ernest Holmes devotes an entire chapter in his book, The Science of Mind, to the Law

---

2 Esther and Jerry Hicks, *The Law of Attraction* (Carlsbad, CA: Hay House, 2000), 32.

of Attraction, and his original text was written in 1926 and revised in 1938. None of this is new information. Holmes said, *"Change your thinking, change your life."*[3] The purpose of the Clarity Concepts™ Model will assist you in understanding:

- **What you ARE thinking and thus ASKING**
- **What do you WANT to be thinking**
- **What thoughts are in your way and creating OBSTACLES**

Many New Thought teachers speak these days about the *imposter syndrome*, especially for women. The research shows men will often move into a career position beyond their current skill set, while women wait until they are overqualified to move up. This is a great example of a thought pattern that could be holding you back from your success.

Just before the COVID-19 shutdown in 2020, I attended a service at the Center for Spiritual Living (CSL) in Palm Desert, California, and two people in the congregation told me the teaching they received there *SAVED Their LIVES*. It may save yours as well if you practice the steps outlined in the following text. During Covid, I joined a remote Zoom meditation group from CSL Palm Desert, which has certainly enhanced my life! The group helped me get through a year of stress. I'm eager to share with you from all I've learned.

The process is straightforward, yes, but not easy. We all have many years of societal views, family patterns, parental guidance, and painful experiences to uncover and unravel before we can get to our true thoughts and have a healthy relationship with ourselves and others. Some believe we also have genetic memory dating to our ancestors. That is, those who came before us created subconscious thought patterns that carry through from generation to generation along the bloodline. In my own life, for example, there is a disturbing pattern in my family of my siblings and me being falsely accused. It has happened so many times that there must be an ancient prototype. This falls under the Holmes' premise of *unconscious invitation*. More on that later . . .

The important differentiation of the Clarity Concepts™ Path for Positive Living Model is that it will push you forward to take actions to support your

---

3 Ernest Holmes, *Change Your Thinking, Change Your Life: A Practical Course in Successful Living* (Los Angeles: Science of Mind Publishing, 1984).

goals. The purpose of the model is to help you commit to your life, your dreams, and your path forward.

It is important to understand that we can be human and imperfect and then self-correct. We all are, after all, masterpieces but works in progress. My goal with this book is to share with you how to resonate at a higher, clearer frequency that raises the vibration of your life. This teaching is centered on the belief that *like attracts like.* Clear energy brings events, people, circumstances, and opportunities into your life in a much easier and more noticeable way. This book is a consolidation of more than 26 years of studying business, psychology and spirituality. I can't wait for you to try out my blended approach.

The Clarity Concepts™ model works for me. My business is booming. (Please do not share this with my ex-husband!) I have confidence it will work for you, too!

The Clarity Concepts™ Model suggests that, especially when we experience repetitive experiences, we are *thinking* something subconsciously. That is, we do not realize or recognize our patterns in thought. For example, I have a history of attracting people into my life who are needy, because I grew up taking care of others. Ernest Holmes calls this *unconscious invitation.* This means that we are inviting experiences into our lives through conscious or unconscious thoughts and emotions.

Holmes suggests unearthing these subconscious thoughts and patterns:

> *When you first start to get your garden ready you are likely to find that it contains a good many stones, weeds, hard chunks of earth, or rubbish. These need to be cleaned away if the soil is to produce as you desired. Similarly, old complexes, attitudes, habits certainly will ruin your harvest in the spiritual realm unless you get them out.*[4]

I was watching *The Bachelor* and was struck by the unchosen woman who cried, "*This ALWAYS happens to me.*" Her statement tells us that unconsciously, she was expecting rejection and thus attracted the exact circumstance into her life. Clarity Concepts™ helps us understand that there is some pattern this bachelorette has developed and so repeatedly falls for men who are not a suitable match for her.

---

4 Reverend Jessee Jones, *The Essential Ernest Holmes,* (New York, NY: Tarcher Putnam, 2002) p. 86

As one motivational speaker advised, you date or marry *the same person, different body* until you change your approach and thought processes. Another way of saying this is that we experience the same life lessons until we finally uproot the core belief and move above and beyond the current situation.

Merely thinking about your goals, without taking action or discovering and rooting out contradictory beliefs, does not ensure success. Desire plus decision equals demonstration!

Too many of us have been given a birthright of negativity. We have been told that life on earth is difficult and arduous, and we should be content with the *pursuit of happiness*. If you add the daily news to your psyche, how can you possibly focus on anything positive? When I was visiting potential private schools for my son, I was impressed by the headmaster at St. Aloysius Academy who regularly asked her students, "What can you do today that is GREAT?" (Of course, I chose that school!) The purpose of this work is to provide the right coaching so you can find happiness through your greatness and not just simply let life happen. Les Brown, the famous motivational speaker, said:

"You don't have to be great to get started, but you have to get started to be great!"

The Clarity Concepts™ coaching model certainly does not mean you should have the expectation to be happy every minute of your day. Life is full of the pairs of opposites, and they cycle as birth/death, positive/negative, summer/winter, yin/yang, and happy/sad. It is very important that you feel and express your emotions.

If you can become CLEAR© on your contribution to the reality occurring in your life, you can even approach a negative or sad experience with a positive attitude. You recognize that even in the midst of difficult of times, your personal evolution and growth is being served. Quite simply, learn from your losses and trust in Spirit. When my brother was falsely accused and arrested, my prayer was that the positive outcome would be his leaving his abusive marriage. I knew it was a wake-up call, and it was!

The key to unlocking your thinking is to acknowledge your emotions and embrace them. Many times, I have experienced extreme sadness but was still able to find happiness in the process. (And sometimes not.) We have been taught to block those emotional expressions labeled as uncomfortable or unacceptable. I once asked a minister friend, "Are you always happy?" He laughed and replied, "Sometimes, I'm happy; sometimes, I feel sad, but at the core of who I am is joy."

I read that our thoughts are electrically processed while our emotions are chemically processed. Thus, our emotions are slower and tend to get backed up. Have you ever wondered why you were sad when you finally took a mini-break or a vacation? Very likely, your emotional responses were simply the backlog you had yet to process. I am a firm believer that unprocessed emotions are a contributor to illness. Taking time to really discern how you are in relationship to your world can heal a cancer diagnosis. A lecturer I heard recently said that cancer is anger turned inward. Anger changes nothing in the physical reality; it is only a catalyst for change.

I want you to know that you have the right to feel angry, sad, depressed, or melancholy. These are all part of our human experience. If you deny these rising emotions, you are denying the essence of yourself. We do not deny these feelings; we deny the power they have over us. Being angry, for instance, is a lifelong experience. Feeling angry has a beginning and an end. Eckhart Tolle then tells us to investigate the anger. Do you criticize a child for expressing appropriate emotion? I also believe, and there is research to support this belief, that *unexpressed emotions can and often do create illness*. Instead of ignoring these emotions, this program will teach you not to alienate and hide them, but to EXPRESS them constructively. This will clear the way for your path to become straight and productive at the same time.

Get ready to unlock the answers to these questions and more:

- What is it I really want?
- What are my fears?
- How do I know what I want or what my decision should be?
- Am I ready to accept a gracious and easily flowing life?
- How am I preventing my good from happening?

Living a conscious life is the way of continually being aware of your thoughts, your feelings, the sensations in your body and your connection to the Universal Force. You may or may not believe in God, but I trust you do believe in something that gave you life. It is this Life Force, which provides us with the power to create. Many call it God. The more conscious we are, the more connected with our Life Force, and the more powerful we become. I'm thankful for the friend who years ago introduced me to the work of Ken Keyes and his *Handbook to Higher Consciousness*.[5] The author clearly illustrates that we have a choice in how we respond and react to life.

Ernest Holmes believes that our Life Force (God) only knows how to say "*YES!*" to whatever idea I place in subconscious mind. Here are some examples:

Thought or Statement	Response of the Universe	Result
My life is a mess.	Yes, it is!	Chaos
My life is peaceful.	Yes, it is!	Peace

The subconscious mind cannot take a joke. It is the servant of your conscious mind and is the direct conduit to the forces of the universe. What you think is what you get. Therefore, I prescribe taking a daily mental inventory of your thoughts, giving your mind a rest through meditation, and checking in with your body, which has its own mind to determine where your focus lies. There is scientific research that the heart makes decisions independent of the brain. When you are aware of all these different aspects of yourself, operating much like a Microsoft Windows environment simultaneously, you are conscious.

When we are conscious, we honor our true desires. We don't separate from ourselves from our Life Force. That is, we do what serves us best. How many times have you been influenced to violate your own desires by a person or a group? The more conscious we are, the better able we become to honor ourselves and what is best for us. Being conscious means finding balance and your own rhythm of life. It means leaving unhealthy, negative, or perhaps even dangerous environments. The true way to be in consciousness is to be in the present. I like to describe consciousness as being true to your heart's desire and "not joining the other team."

Let yourself be silently drawn by the gentle pull of what you really love. ~Rumi

5 Ken Keyes, *Handbook to Higher Consciousness* (Berkeley, CA: Living Love Center, 1974).

Through Clarity You Become Conscious

It is in taking actions congruent with our stated desires that we maintain clarity and move into a conscious life. For most of us, our desires can be hard to unearth, and that's why the Clarity Concepts™ method is so important to supporting a conscious life. Listen to that still, small voice within you. To achieve connection to the still, small voice, meditation and yoga are recommended so you can slow down. If you are so busy, you can't hear the message!

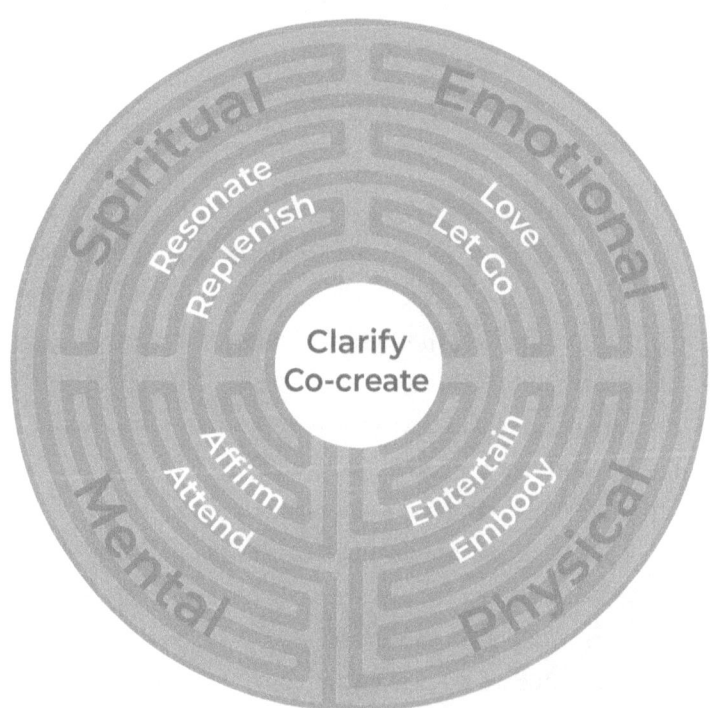

THE CLARITY CONCEPTS™ MODEL

This model is built on the acronym C.L.E.A.R.

C – Clarify, Co-Creation

Clarify: Be clear on exactly what you are seeking in your life; examine your thoughts both conscious and subconscious. Clue: To uncover your subconscious thoughts, look at what is happening in your life.

Co-Creation: Know that you have the power to **create** a brighter and better outcome in your life. Also, learn to **love** what is in your life so you can move forward.

L – Love, Letting Go

Love: Love everything in your life; trust that even the painful experiences are here to support you and move you forward. The painful experiences offer growth opportunities.

Letting Go: The key to **letting go** is forgiveness; you can't move to a new house without leaving the old home. Resentment and holds us back because we are resending the same messages over and over again.

E – Embody, Entertain

Embody: Make sure you are taking the actions that support your future. I made a commitment that Pilates was good for me and the key to my good health; I have not missed a week in the three years since I made the commitment. Also, new research shows that it takes much longer than three weeks to develop a positive habit. Give yourself time to create new habits!

Entertain: Think BIG and **entertain** concepts of a better reality for you. Write down your goals and put them in a safe place. You don't have to share your plans with anyone.

A – Affirm, Attend

Affirm: Using **affirmations** is one of the best ways to redirect your subconscious beliefs. Give yourself positive messaging to help you move past the current relationships and situations you are attracting.

Attend: Pay **attention** to what you are thinking and clear your mind of negative thoughts. Additionally, pay **attention** to where you are spending your time. Are you committed to the outcomes you desire? Also pay **attention** to what is happening in your life, your body, and relationships. What needs to change?

R – Resonate, Replenish

Resonate: Generate and share great energy through gifting. Give to others and spend time with those who are positive and supportive of you. Engage in positive activities. Set clear boundaries with everyone!

Replenish: Take time for self-care. Watch what you eat and drink, and take stock of your wellness activities. Spend time in nature.

The model described in this book will teach you how to achieve anything you desire.

The process is simple:

- **Decide what you want (Clarify/Co-Create)**
- **Discover and the root out your negative beliefs (Love/Let Go/Attend)**
- **Believe in your goal (Affirm/Entertain)**
- **Take actions toward your goal (Embody)**
- **Let go and let it happen as you raise your positive vibrations (Resonate/ Replenish)**

This requires you believe anything is possible; anything can change or be healed. Who thought the Berlin Wall would ever come down? Clearly, many people held on to the positive vision of the reunification of Germany.

Decide: This universal process is simple, yet it is not always easy. For some, making decisions is difficult. If you believe one choice precludes another, you may hold on to a multitude of conflicting desires thus creating confusing choices in your life.

Discover: Observe what appears in your life and look inside to uncover subconscious and or negative beliefs attracting the exact opposite of what you are seeking. There are many ways to do this, which we will explore in depth as we move through the exercises for each step of the CC model.

Believe: Look at the friends and role models you deem successful. Watch how they make clear-cut choices in their lives. Can you think of anyone who overcame obstacles to achieve success? The first person I think of is Nelson Mandela. He never let go of his belief that he would be released from prison and could eliminate the apartheid policies in South Africa. Remember, this happened as a result of the physical action of embargoes of South African goods.

Take Action: You must also align your actions with your desires. If you wish to relocate to California, buying a new home in Oklahoma may interfere with your future outcome. Take care in your actions as they, too, contribute to your requests of the Universe.

Let Go: Your thought processes contribute to what appears in your life. Thus, if your thoughts are negative, doubtful, and untrusting, this is what you create. Your life will be fraught with difficulty, mistrust, and lack of ease. The sooner you recognize your own personal power and let go of the past, the sooner you can get your life on the track you choose.

And sometimes, things happen to turn your course in life. Instead of resisting them, embrace them as opportunities for change. And, of course, let go of whatever is in your way.

So, start at the beginning. Clear your mind of negative patterns. Train your brain to act with laser-like precision to select your choices in life.

Let go of all the negative emotions that interfere with your choices:

- Guilt and Shame
- Doubt and Fear
- Blame, Self-Blame, and Regret
- Greed, Lust, Gluttony, Wrath, Sloth
- Envy and Pride (aka the Seven Deadly Sins)

Instead, let's replace these with:

- Trust and Focus
- Love and Calm
- Ease and Knowing
- Faith and Surrender
- Power

Okay, you might be thinking, *I have already tried to do all this*!

Great! Then you are ready for Clarity Concepts™ as it provides a multidirectional and multidimensional approach to designing your life and bringing you closer to trusting and loving your life.

All the work you have done up to this point supports you in your efforts to enhance your life.

Understanding where you are putting your thoughts is your first step.

Harvard researcher Shawn Achor labeled this work as creating a Happiness Advantage, and wrote a book with that title.[6] I like to call the approach **"problem-solving with Spirit."**

You got this!

As we move forward in the book, I explain how you have the power to create the desired outcomes in your life. My personal life stories show that one simple thought manifests a result or a solution very quickly. This comes after years of practice, but if you simply believe in an outcome, then the thought is answered without interference.

As we begin to understand the power or our thoughts, desires, requests, actions, and directions, we begin to realize how thought energy affects the physical body. This work is well documented in Masaru Emoto's *The Hidden Messages in Water*. His research captured crystalline photos of water after his research team sent specific thoughts and energy to the water. The results are amazing, and I recommend this book as you travel on this journey. This is the picture of the water's change after prayers and positive energy were sent to it[7].

Well Done   Let's do it!

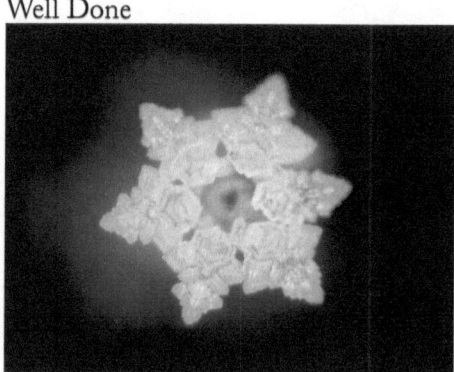

6 Shawn Achor, *The Happiness Advantage* (New York: Random House, 2010).
7 (C) Office Masaru Emoto, LLC also Masaru Emoto, *The Hidden Messages in Water* (New York: Atria Books, 2011).

Do it! You Fool

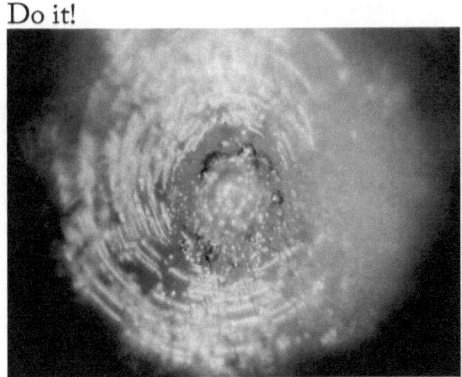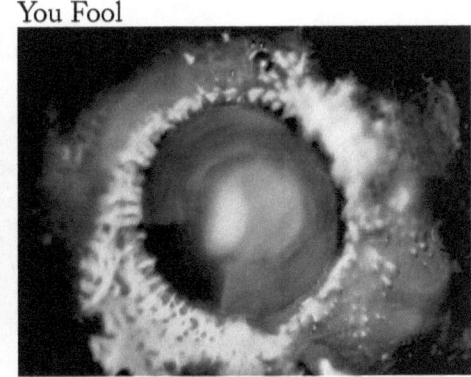

The pictures above illustrate how negativity changes the physical as does positivity. Notice the changes in your life as you begin to emphasize the positive. What is more subtle is the difference in the water structure between *Do It* as a command, which looks harsh, versus *Let's Do It* as a team, which looks much more positive and embracing.

There are many ways to actively embrace positive energy in your life. The most important one is taking the time to stop, to let your emotions process, to get in touch with your true feelings, and not the "shoulds" imposed on us by the world view.

In the next chapters, we look at each of the steps in the Clarity Concepts™ for Positive Living model.

Clarity Synonyms

Elucidate
Make Clear
Explain
Illuminate
Spell Out
Simplify
Refine

Clarity Antonyms

Cloud
Puzzle
Perplex
Baffle
Muddle
Bewilder
Confound
Complicate
Blur
Confuse

STEP ONE: CLARITY

"Clarity is the source of authentic leadership and high performance. It allows us to be present in the moment and have an enjoyable experience of life. A sense of purpose, direction, and entrepreneurial spirit are natural for people with a clear head." ~Jamie Smart[8]

A plaque in my office reads, *Will this matter a year from now?* This echoes the work of Stephen R. Covey, a famous leadership expert. Every thought or word we place in our lives affects the outcomes we experience. Therefore, if you are seeking to have a new experience, you need to focus your mind and take movement in the right direction.

Have you ever undergone one of those moments when you just KNEW what your next step was going to be? Once you are clear on where you want to head in life, the rest falls easily into place. Because I was clear on what I was seeking in a partner, I knew Ron was the man I was waiting for. After each step in the Clarity Concepts™ model, I will share my relevant stories.

Reflect back on a time when you set a goal and it came into being. To obtain crystal clear vision of your goals, sometimes you have to seek guidance from Spirit. If you pray, then pray. If you don't know where you are heading, pray for clarity. Ask Spirit, God, Jesus, Mohamed, or the Universe for clarity and crystal-clear direction. Don't put pressure on yourself, take a break treat this moment in life as if you have just let go of the trapeze and have not yet connected with the next rung. You can reinvent yourself!

What happens if you don't like what you have created?

I was fortunate to hear prosperity teacher, Edwene Gaines, speak many years ago. She told a story about how she set a dream in motion to move into a posh

---

8 Jamie Smart, *The Little Book of Clarity* (West Sussex, UK: Wiley and Sons, 2015).

large white mansion. Sometime after she set this goal, she moved into that exact house. In her telling the story, I imagined it as an Antebellum-style Colonial with six bedrooms, each with its own ensuite bathroom, a large entry way with a magnificent chandelier, and a long tree-lined driveway. Edwene told us she was only in the residence for a few months when she realized she was not happy in her large white house. Instead of clinging to something she was dissatisfied with, she sold the house and moved into her next dream house. Something similar happened to me three times when starting a new job. Within a month, I knew it was time for a change, and I immediately made it happen.

Many of us don't move forward because we are afraid to make the wrong decision. Therefore, we don't go anywhere. If you tell the Universe you are "unsure," then the Universe confirms these feelings for you. Confusing choices then come your way further energizing your indecision.

Please, please make a choice and move forward with the consequences. If you don't like what you achieve, you are already one step further towards your dreams, because now you can eliminate a choice. The more choices you can eliminate, the closer you are to **clarifying** your true desire. That is the point of **co-creation**; when you know mentally, emotionally, physically, and spiritually exactly what it is you are seeking, your experience changes, and you demonstrate accordingly.

I am writing this at a time when I am examining some of the realities I created in my own life. I wrote part of this section in a café at a ski resort in the snowy Austrian Alps. Please take note that when I worked on what I wanted my future partnership to look like I wrote "European-Minded." On paper, and in the fabulous photographs, this appears to be a dream vacation. However, I dislike cold and snow, and I despise long car rides. My first husband kept telling me to emphasize the positive sides of the trip. Yes, the thermal baths were great, the Thai massage in Budapest was award-winning, and the Austrian food tremendous, yet, as I examine my emotions, I feel sad. I gained clarity that some things in my life must change.

When we are clear on our heart's desire, changes come easily to us. It is like the voice in the movie "*Field of Dreams.*" "If you build it, they will come."[9] This means that you need to do the work around what it is you truly want. The work involves

---

9 Kevin Costner, "Field of Dreams," directed by Phil Alden Robinson, Universal Pictures, 1989.

becoming clear on what you want: good health, money, and/or a relationship. Therefore, if something is in the way of good health, like smoking, this habit may no longer be appealing to you. With clarity, you can conquer anything.

So how do we become clear? We set a bull's-eye on what we want. If you are seeking a new partner, write down the attributes you desire. If you are seeking a new job, write down the skill sets that you want to utilize. Be clear about how much money you want to earn and the environment in which you want to work. Job attributes could include great use of my _____ skills. Let's fill in the blank:

- Coaching skills
- Writing skills
- Communication skills
- Team building skills
- Technical skills, etc.

You do not want to be overly specific as you want to leave room for something even greater than what you may imagine.

I know that denying the sadness and other emotions I felt in the Austrian Alps only creates illness and discontent if left to fester. What I chose to do in that moment is process my feelings and make a plan for the future so that I am confident my next trip will be easier. I may even choose to skip such a ski trip in the future. For God's sake, I don't ski! On the other hand, this was a trip of a lifetime; we saw some beautiful sights, and my son got to spend precious time with his cousins. Recently, I traveled to Banff, Alberta, Canada, for my niece's wedding and used the Austrian trip as the prototype of what not to do! The Banff trip was a huge success!

I also got to work on one of my core issues on the Austrian trip. Ever since I was young, I have been afraid of being trapped. It may stem from being stuck in a closet in my childhood home on Long Island because of a broken lock. On this Austrian trip, I was trapped in an airplane, trapped in a car ride on snowy roads for seven hours, stuck with a stepdaughter who clearly was irritated by my presence, and stuck in a cold restaurant where no one spoke English while the others skied. As I lived through each experience, I felt stronger and freer. In this process, I am also uncovering some **Clarity** I have been seeking for some time; there is some separation I need to **Create.**

Get ready to unlock the answers to these questions and more:

- What is it I really want?
- What are my fears?
- How do I know what I want or what my decision should be?
- Am I ready to accept a gracious and easily flowing life?
- How am I preventing my good from happening?
- Then, make a decision—no worries, you can always change your mind later.

Clarity Story: A Brand-New Practical Car

I gave up my Audi for a practical Saturn. Boy, was that a BIG mistake! I learned:

- Make sure you have all repair work on Euro Cars done at the dealer.
- Drive what you **love** because you spend a lot of time in your car.
- Don't buy something you think is "practical" when you want something else.
- Know that you deserve luxury.

The Audi had some serious problems. However, I am now convinced that if I hadn't worried about money and taken it to the Audi dealership, the problems could have been resolved under warranty. My Audi may have been more financially prudent than the new car I purchased.

I bought a Saturn as they were reasonably priced and did not haggle in the dealership. Dealerships were scary to me at the time, and even so, I went by myself. I chose a Saturn so I would not be taken advantage of. I disliked the Saturn from the day I brought it home! What was I thinking, trading down from my beautiful Audi? And the car turned out to be impractical. Not long after I purchased it, I hit a curb in a rainstorm and blew a tire; the accident ruined a rim. After the repair, every time I started the car, a loud, scary noise would erupt. Shortly after I purchased the car, I took the Saturn back to the dealership for a recall; this gave me another data point, proving the inadequacy of this vehicle. The Saturn dealership could not find the noise emanating from the wheel well. Ultimately, I went to another dealership, when the clutch blew early, and they discovered that a plastic mount in the wheel well was missing. Finally, the horrific noise was gone! I took the successful repair as a sign from the that I could sell the car.

I wanted a luxury car, and, since buying a new car had been a complete failure, I chose to buy a pre-owned luxury car. My sights were set on a Toyota Avalon as they just came on the market. My brother works for a Toyota dealership, so I trusted the brand and the service I would receive. He connected me with John, one of the salesmen on the dealership's used car lot. I met with John and told him I was looking for a pre-owned Avalon. John agreed it was a great car, but he warned me that I may not find one on the secondary market because they were still in their first model year. I said, "Okay, but an Avalon is what I want." I was clear on what I was seeking. I was also willing to be patient now that my Saturn was running smoothly.

My brother called to ask me how the car search was going, and I let him know John was not very optimistic about finding me a pre-owned Avalon. My brother said, "Why don't you get a Toyota Camry with the V-6-cylinder engine? It is essentially the exact same car." I stored this information away.

John called me from the dealership about two weeks later. John's follow-up call is an interesting lesson in great sales techniques. John said, "I'm just checking in with you. As I predicted, we have not had an Toyota Avalon come in on the used car lot."

"That's okay," I said. "Do you happen to have any Camrys with the upgraded engine?"

"Let, me check, but I doubt it." Then he added with surprise, "Why yes, we do. We just had a Camry XLE (Extra Luxury Edition) come in yesterday."

"Great," I said, "I'm coming out to see it." I purchased my ruby red car - I named her "Valentine" - with the gray leather interior and the upgraded V-6 engine. My friend referred to it as my new "condo." The Camry was a bargain because it was three years old with little mileage on it. The car was in impeccable condition! Valentine and I were together for many years. She, along with my Guardian Angel, protected me when I was hit by a semi-trailer on the New Jersey Turnpike heading for the Holland Tunnel. I kept her for over 120,000 miles until the windows would not go up on a rainy drive to New York City. Then I knew it was time for a new vehicle. I drove luxury Volvos for years and will share with you the stories of my post-Volvo cars later.

There are a number of great lessons and examples in this story:

1. Be clear and precise about what you are seeking.
2. Be patient and make space for your vision to become clear.
3. Be flexible, Spirit may have a better answer for you.

4. Be persistent. The used car salesman did not think he had a car for me, but he called anyway.
5. Know that comfort doesn't have to be extravagant.
6. Don't settle for less than what your heart desires.

Clarity Story: My First Home Purchase

When I was 29, my company asked me to transfer back to my hometown of Philadelphia. I was thrilled! Around the same time, I thought I was in love with someone who was living in a developing country far away and hard to reach. I planned to visit him at great expense, yet, I kept thinking I should buy a house, too. I went ahead and purchased a ticket to travel to see him and twice it was cancelled by the airlines. The Universe spoke loudly that I should not make this journey. Eventually, I got the **Clarity** that he was not communicating with me, and I ended our discussions about me coming to meet him. Instead, I went to Key West and enjoyed a memorable vacation before I started my new position. When I returned, off I went to purchase a home. I required three simple structural requests:

1. A ceramic tile kitchen floor
2. A large deck for entertaining
3. A low-maintenance exterior and of course within my price range

I also drew a circle on the map about halfway way between my hometown of Meadowbrook and my new job in Malvern. My realtor kept insisting I needed to move to a condominium. I was not so sure. The day we began our search, her office listed a newly renovated older home, and she showed me the photo. It was rather unappealing, but my mom suggested it needed landscaping to spruce up the curb appeal, and we decided to see it. The minute I walked in, I knew it was my house when I saw the ceramic tile in the front porch and kitchen. The deck was new and massive, and the house had been completely renovated with vinyl siding and new windows. The home was located in the geographic area I identified. I made an offer that day and lived very happily in that home for 12 years until I met my first husband. Living in that house, I enjoyed the friendship of many people and am glad I listened to my heart and not to what the Realtor thought was best for me.

Ultimately, I made a great profit on the house, and it helped me obtain the home I am in now, which I adore and reminds me of homes in New Orleans where I was born.

Clarity Story: Asilomar Conference Grounds

The Centers for Spiritual Living (CSL), formerly called The Church of Religious Science, founded by Ernest Holmes, used to have a two-week spiritual conference every summer in Pacific Grove, CA., at the tip of the Monterey Peninsula. It was held at the Asilomar State Conference Grounds. The architect of the original buildings was Julia Morgan who, incidentally, was also the architect of Hearst Castle. The grounds are incredible as all the structures are made from old redwood and the site is on higher ground, just across from Pebble Beach, overlooking the Monterey Bay. Just the smell of the ocean and redwoods transports me back to this beautiful, sacred site.

I decided one year that I was going to go to Asilomar. At the time, I did not know that Asilomar was the name of the Conference Center, not the actual CSL conference. I invested in a sound energy healing system and the group announced they were holding a conference on healing through Light, Sound, and Color at Asilomar. There it was. I was going to Asilomar!

The conference was amazing. While there, we were blessed to see a comet in the sky over Monterey Bay. The stories on the Aramaic translations of the Bible were fascinating, and there was much healing in the sound and color sessions. I enjoyed an incredible experience there.

The next year, I was teaching the **Clarity Concepts™** model at the Center for Spiritual Living in the Philadelphia area, and I saw the flyer for the CSL Asilomar Conference Center. I looked at it and thought, *If I had the right room-mate, I would attend this conference.* I no sooner finished saying this to myself when one of my students walked over to me and said, "Would you be my roommate at Asilomar?" I barely interacted with her in the class, but off to Asilomar we went, and we were best friends for almost two decades.

Two years later, once my labyrinths were created, I was invited to run a laby-rinth program at the CSL Asilomar Conference. As a result, I have spent over 100 precious days of my life on those conference grounds sharing healing labyrinth experiences.

Clarity Exercises

I. <u>Self-Speak</u>: **For the next week, create a journal page on negative thoughts; write down anything you say to yourself that is negative and lacking in faith.**

Watch for thoughts of: *Frustration, Stuck in a Hole, Helplessness.* While doing this work, I discovered my tendency to criticize my spending habits. Other seminar participants questioned their parenting skills and their futures. I suggest adding an affirmation when you identify a negative thought. For me, my affirmation read like this: **I live in an abundant and prosperous Universe, and all my needs are met.** We will work on affirmations in future weeks in the **Affirm** step of the CC model.

The purpose of this exercise is to help you dig deeper into the underlying messages you are giving to yourself and help you get in touch with your true nature. We will use this work later on in the model to help create positive affirmations.

II. **Create your own special daily prayer**

Use this as a mantra when something is upsetting you; use it in traffic to stay calm; use it when facing conflict:

What is it that is calling me today?
I am a child of God in whom he/she is well pleased.
I am happy, joyous, and free in my thinking.
The Universe is always supporting me.
I am surrendering to my best life, or my perfect life, or my desired life.

III. **Dream Big, Turn It Over: What is it you want to place in the hands of Spirit this week?**

In the early stages of learning this work, you can set goals but try to make them very general. The reason you don't want to be extremely specific right now is so that Spirit can contribute to the result. Sometimes the Universal Force has a much greater idea in mind than you can think! Your wishes could be as expansive as owning a plane, becoming a millionaire, or simply living a happy, healthy, quiet life.

IV. **Journal page on "Turning It Over." What is too big for you to imagine? Do you need to raise your "glass ceiling of receptivity"?**

Write down your big dreams - create a list of things you desire in life that might be above your "glass ceiling" of receptivity and are currently a little too big for you to imagine.

- Career:
- Family:
- Lifestyle:
- Income:
- Home Residence:
- Vacations:
- Friends:
- Activities:
- Passions:
- Partnerships:

Creation Synonyms
Make
Sustain
Generate
Produce
Fashion
Invent
Initiate
Originate

Creation Antonyms
Obliteration
Annihilation
Devastation
Demolition
Ruin
Damage

STEP TWO: CO-CREATION

Leadership Expert Stephen Covey advises:

> Begin with the End in Mind is based on the principle that all things are created twice. There's a mental or first creation and a physical or second creation to all things.[10]

This book is about the Universal Power that you have to make things happen in your life. You simply need to establish the connection.

Co-Creation is the understanding that there is a Power for good in this Universe, and you can use it. Simply put, if there is something you desire and it is for your highest good, you can achieve this goal through thoughtful action and thoughtful consciousness. Where this coaching method differs from others is the focus on action and making sure the steps you are taking in life are congruent with your goals. The reason **Clarity** is first is because when you are clear on what you desire, you are more likely to attract what it is you are seeking. Some call this the Law of Attraction, which we will discuss in other steps. The Law of Attraction is a universal process through which you attract relationships, situations, and results aligned with your energy. Simply put, consciousness helps you to separate from what you are most familiar with and help you to align with something greater than the experiences you have had to date. (Failed marriage, unemployment, illness,

---

10 Stephen R. Covey, *The 7 Habits of Highly Effective People* (New York: Simon and Schuster, 2020), 113.

death, etc.) To help you further understand, I will share some of my **Co-creation** experiences when it came to envisioning my professional success.

In a tough situation ask yourself empowering questions: *What is trying to emerge in my life? What is my gift to share?* Stop asking yourself, *What's wrong? Why me?* These are disempowering statements! Then listen and be available to make the necessary adjustments.

The **Co-Creation** step is actually a philosophy. You know in your heart you have the power to create positive outcomes in your life. How do you do this?

- **Decide what you want**
- **Believe in your goal**
- **Take action towards your goal and let it happen.**

You must also believe anything is possible; anything can change or be healed. For example, whoever thought the Berlin Wall would come down or apartheid would end? Hold on to those visions! Your visions may be smaller in comparison, but they are no less important.

Decide: The universal process is simple, yet it is not always easy. For some, making decisions is difficult. If you believe one choice precludes another, you may hold onto a multitude of conflicting desires thus creating confusing choices in your life. There is an old joke about five frogs sitting on a log. One decides to jump off. How many frogs are on the log? (It's a trick question!) Five. Deciding is only part of the equation; acting is the second component.

Believe: Look at your friends and role models who you deem successful. Watch how they make clear-cut choices in their lives. Can you think of anyone who overcame obstacles to achieve success? The first person I think of is Nelson Mandela. He never let go of his belief that he would ultimately be released from prison and could release his country of South Africa from their discriminatory policies of apartheid. Even more astounding, he was elected President!

Align: You must also align your actions with your desires. If you wish to relocate to California, buying a new home in Nebraska may interfere with your future outcome. Take care in your actions as they, too, contribute to your requests of the Universe. Be watchful as to how you treat others; your actions are magnified and returned to you. Rabbi Marc Gaffni said, *Never let a person serve you whose name you do not know.*

Spiritual Prayer as the Way to Co-Create

Co-Creation is the process of working with Spirit, creating what is best for you in your life. Find your way to work with God or Spirit, Walk in Nature, sing hymns, go to church, pray as you were taught. Use the prayer treatment taught by Ernest Holmes as follows:

1. *Recognition*: God is all there is.
2. *Identification*: I am one with God. I am a drop of water in the ocean of consciousness that is God. I contain all the qualities of God, but I am not all of God.
3. *Affirmation or Declaration*: The home I desire is awaiting my recognition of it. I take the necessary steps to investigate real estate in the neighborhood of my choice, and I find the right and perfect home.
4. *Thanksgiving*: I joyfully receive and give thanks for the gifts God bestows upon me as I am open and receptive to God's living spirit of Truth.
5. *Release and Acceptance*: I release my word to the activity of the Law of Mind, knowing God in Its infinite wisdom knows what is for my highest and best. And so, it is. Amen.[11]

And we always say our desired intention manifests or something even better we could not imagine arrives. That is the key to manifestation/demonstration - accept what shows up in your life and let go of what you expected to happen. Ernest Holmes said, "Always expect the best."

And, you do not have to use this type of prayer. Use the prayers you learned in childhood such as "The Lord's Prayer." Researcher Larry Dossey[12] has documented the power and healing properties of prayer.

Look at your list of desires and see if you can identify the motivation or driving force behind what it is you are seeking. For example, why do you want to be

---

11 Reverend Jessee Jones, *The Essential Ernest Holmes*, (New York, NY: Tarcher Putnam, 2002) p. 36

12 Larry Dossey, *Healing Words: The Power of Prayer and the Practice of Medicine* (New York: HarperCollins, 1993).

successful? Is it because you don't want to be afraid? If a goal is driven by fear, you may have conflicting thought patterns interfering with your manifesting your desires. Make sure you look for other positive motivators. For me, I have been working from home for 26 years, so when I pivoted my business, it led me into an area of insurance work that allowed me to continue to work from home. This was my priority. I could have gotten a desk or sales job, but I wanted to continue my lifestyle and create time to motivate others. Do try to get to the underlying emotion and drive behind your desires.

A note on co-creation:

Remain gentle with yourself as you begin to assume responsibility for the occurrences in your life. For instance, if you break your leg, please don't beat yourself up. A friend of mine kept telling people, "I need a break." The subconscious mind can't take a joke, and Charles stepped off a curb at the supermarket while looking ahead to see where he parked his car and broke his hip and leg which laid him up for four months. Instead, take the time to explore why this may have happened. Is it time to change directions? Take time to emphasize the positive and look for a silver lining! Charles' blessing in his recuperation was him having the time to write his memoir.

Co-Creation Story: The Universe's School Plan for My Son

I was sharing my story with a new friend at our swim club as to how Spirit guided me to enroll my son in Catholic school. Wendy pulled close and said, "I love God stories!"

The story begins when I moved my son from the private nursery school at our Episcopal church to public school for kindergarten. Some friends spent a year at our local public elementary school and then opted back to private school. Before school even began, I managed to upset the public school principal so much that he called and yelled at me for insisting our schedule required morning kindergarten. I painstakingly crafted my son's new school plan, and this man threatened to interfere with my plan and with my ability to work and support my family. If not for the support of my first husband, I would have pulled Mackie from the public school before kindergarten even started. But part of marriage is compromise and patience, and my son knew many friends in his morning public kindergarten, so we stayed on our course. My son's academic abilities strengthened being in kindergarten twice a day, and we enjoyed a wonderful school year.

A few months later, a neighbor boy who attended public school confided in me that he was not getting breakfast. There had been a recent death in the family, and I was hesitant to address the family directly due to some prior events. So, I asked the school secretary if I could leave a note for the Guidance Counselor at the front desk in the elementary school. When I made my request, the principal whipped his head around. He challenged me, breaching my privacy, and asked, "Why do you want do that?" Ignoring this major privacy breach, I explained without revealing who the child was, and the principal told me in no uncertain terms that I should address this with the child's mother.

I was extremely uncomfortable doing that, so I discussed it with another neighbor who told me that the school served breakfast. I decided that was enough of a solution, and I gave it no further thought. Apparently, the other neighbor shared my concerns with the boy's mother, and it turns out she went into a dark place, and she actually went and turned herself in to the principal. Really, you can't make this stuff up. Her husband later confronted me on the street while I was with my son, and I had to step out of his way as he was clearly in a rage. When I took that step, I knew instantly we were leaving the public school.

After I told my story, Wendy said, "You were convicted in the heart with the Holy Spirit." If you can follow that conviction, life opens up much more easily for you.

After a long search, we enrolled my son in a private Catholic Academy. I never planned to look at a Christian or Catholic school. I was certain we would find a private school or a Quaker Friends school. A family friend strongly recommended we look at this school, and we liked everything we saw there. Spirit's plan for our family through the Catholic approach has really crafted my son's life in a magnificent way. It has also been very healing for me because I do not have fond memories of my Catholic School experience. My teenage son has a strong faith, is devoted to his church, and rooted in knowing that giving back and treating others with respect is the key to a successful life.

During Mackie's third year with the Academy, the Religious Studies nun pulled me aside and told me that Mackie could not participate in the upcoming First Holy Communion unless we joined a Catholic Church and got a "Catholic

Blessing" of his Episcopal Baptism. My son was baptized on Christmas morning in Grand Rapids, Michigan. It was held in his grandfather's Episcopal church and his Hungarian cousin was baptized with him. I was upset by the thought that somehow his baptism was not adequate. We regularly attended the Episcopal church where my son attended pre-school. The Academy received a copy of this certificate three years prior when we applied in kindergarten. This was extremely short notice. Once again, I had that funny feeling that Mackie might be changing schools again. At the time, this made no sense to me, but I later learned he was not happy with his teacher that year.

Looking for a solution, the first call I made was to an old friend who was the school secretary at the local parish school. She advised that I should call the parish nun and meet with her. She was a St. Joseph's nun; this was the same order I studied under in grade school. I mentioned that she reminded me of my first-grade teacher, Sister Thomas Kathleen. She stared at me and said, "I know her." She immediately signed my paperwork and registered us as parishioners. The parish priest was extremely welcoming and declared that my son's Episcopal baptism was acceptable to the parish. I left the Episcopal church and began to worship at the Catholic church. I toured their school and fell in love with it. We moved Mackie there in fourth grade, and I cannot express how remarkable the school has been for us as a family. I feel blessed to be in their community. That summer, my son made a good friend, who ended up in his class in the fall, and he paved the way for our transition to the new school. If you listen carefully, Spirit always guides you in the right direction. In fact, if I had really listened, I would have moved him right after Christmas. Those productive five years just flew by and he is now in public school with 16 of his classmates from St. Katherine's. He walked into homeroom as a freshman, and four of his SKS friends were in the group. They will be together for four years.

Co-Creation Story: A Cup of Coffee

One Sunday, in the fall, my son's father and I had one of our "Sunday Talks" wherein we discussed marital and parenting issues. We experienced a number of co-parenting issues with my stepdaughters, and I was distressed about the tenor of the conversation. I decided what I needed was a friend to speak with <u>over a good cup of coffee.</u>

I drove to the supermarket to grab some groceries. On my way home, I passed a neighborhood in my town and thought, *I wonder if that is where Mackie's pre-school friend and his family live?* I turned up the street, and there was a little park. At the playground in the park stood my friend watching over her children. She came to the car, noticing I was visibly upset. "Do you want to come in for coffee?" I said, "Yes, of course," as I promptly burst into tears. She brewed one of the best cups of coffee I have ever tasted and helped me to sort through resolving my issues. Spirit clearly led me to turn into her neighborhood and found me support.

Co-Creation Story: My Career Path

One of the ways we **co-create** is by spending the time to write about the goals and expectations we may have around a certain desire. In Advanced Accounting in college, I was given an assignment to write a paper about my career path. I thought it was odd! Instead of having us create a research paper, this professor wanted to know what my plans were for my career. So, I wrote up my plan. I discussed the fact that I was graduating with a double major and was thus presented with a choice. I could go into accounting with my degree and experience as a bookkeeper, and/or I discussed how exciting it would be socially to work for a major accounting firm and travel to clients and learn new businesses. I also thought I would be bored with this career and noted that an accounting position was a second choice for me. My real goal was to get a job in Corporate Risk Management. I noted that the social aspects might not be as fun, but I would find the job more rewarding. There were no entry-level jobs in Philadelphia, and I would most likely have to move to New York. Well, guess what the results were? (Other than the fact that the professor gave me a C-minus on my paper because I did not choose Accounting!)

I was offered a job, after a national search, in Houston, but I was clear that the move would be tough for me, so I asked for two weeks to work on making such a significant change, as I had never been away from my home. I also asked for a week unpaid in the summer to go on vacation at the beach. Their response? They revoked the offer! A great teacher of manifestation, Shakti Gawain, suggests that your request and response to outcomes you are trying to create should be: "I ask for this or something better."[13] At the time their response was so severe, and the interview had been so grueling, I was shaken but happy I did not have to leave the East Coast. Exhausted from my internship, I decided to take the summer off to unwind. In the end, I resumed my job search in September, and I was hired for a great job in New York and an even better one three months after that.

It's important to note that I found the great job in New York by calling one of my professors and asking for help in my job search. He connected me with a placement firm, and I was easily employed in NYC.

Co-Creation Story: A New Job Is Coming to Me

Because of a nightmare boss, the job transfer to Philadelphia proved to be problematic, and ultimately, I moved to another position in the area. However, that job got me back to Philadelphia and introduced me to one of my best friends. I specifically chose the new job because the company had a nice vibe, and I liked my prospective manager whose last name was pronounced, "HUMAN." He was a great guy!

I also chose the job because I knew it would not be a problem for me to leave promptly at 5:00 p.m. two nights a week to attend classes at Rosemont College in their "Holistic Health Perspectives Program." Through a friend I met in this program, I was introduced to the Centers for Spiritual Living and the teachings of Ernest Holmes. I was strongly guided to complete the program, and because I was clear on this, I was able to turn down another more lucrative albeit stressful opportunity.

Two years later, I again found myself dissatisfied with my job. This time it was because of a colleague who was challenging and difficult. I liked my job and was in no hurry to leave, so this time, I handled my job search on a **metaphysical** level. In February of that year, I declared to myself, *A new job is coming to me.* I did not share this intention with anyone. Sometimes, it's best to keep our dreams private, playing our cards close to the chest

I was also clear I would not switch positions until after I spoke at the National Risk Management Conference in Orlando that year. I remained

---

13 Shakti Gawain, *Creative Visualization: Use the Power of Your Imagination to Create What You Want in Your Life* (Novato, CA: New World Library, 2002).

open because I did not know if my next step would be in Risk Management or whether I would make a move into a holistic or wellness career. The Orlando conference was a success, and I came home perplexed. At this point, I did not have one job lead.

The situation at work calmed down, and that summer, I received the opportunity to travel to my employer's German plants. I had a fantastic time as I managed to meet a friend of a friend in Dusseldorf, and in addition, my co-workers were lovely. I was starting to think that I may stay with my current job. Total Quality Management Committee provided a great learning experience, and I enjoyed a nice travel schedule. It was while on the trip to Dusseldorf, I received a voicemail from a college friend that her husband had been recruited to start a Risk Management Consulting department for a Safety Engineering firm. She said, "I keep telling him the job is for you, not for him." I interviewed for the job, received an offer, and gave my 30-day notice, telling my employer I was moving to a consulting role. My new employer was planning on giving me a consulting contract with the firm. While I was wrapping things up during those 30 days, I received a call from another company I supported. "We want to hire you!" That company is still a long-term risk consulting client of mine.

Thus, I received two job offers without interviewing, submitting a resume, or researching the job market. No one knew I was interested in a new position. I simply made a declaration to the Universe, calling these job offers to me. The new job did not last long, however, but it led me to where I ultimately needed to be. Often opportunities are not landing strips; they are launching pads to new and greater experiences.

Co-Creation Story: Manifestation

Years ago, I struggled with the bottom line in my bank account. There was plenty of money in accounts receivable, but no cash in the bank. So, I did what one of my teachers suggested and "put the problem on God's altar." That meant letting go and simply knowing the result I desired is achieved. Nestled in an alcove near my front door, I have a beautiful antique shaker table my first husband purchased years ago. On this table – my altar - are arranged many spiritual artifacts, including Quan Yin, Chinese Goddess of Compassion and Mercy, Archangel Michael, the Protector, Spiritual Art, Icons of Saints and the Blessed Mother from around the world, Our Lady of Guadalupe, crystals, photos, and other talismans. Underneath a Celtic circle, I placed a note that simply read "cash flow." I thought, *yes, that is what I need, cash flowing in.*

Within minutes, the phone rang, and it was the manager of my local Trader Joe's calling to tell me I had won a bag of groceries. Ten minutes later, a large law firm called to confirm a major interview for a huge project. And two days after that, I won a raffle with prizes and gift cards worth over $200! Next time, I intend to be more specific. I could have asked for more!

Evidence of Co-creation: Stories of Synchronicity

The Voicemail

Recently, I called to confirm an appointment with my chiropractor. It was odd, they were not picking up the phone. I Googled their office, and realizing the number in my phone contacts was one digit off, I corrected it in my phone contacts. Then, I got a call from an unidentified caller, and I texted, *Can I call you later?* The caller responded, *Sure.* I then asked, "Who are you?" And he replied, "I am the contractor who worked for you years ago in North Wildwood." I had been looking for a contractor, and here he was!

Jersey Shore Encounter

We were in Stone Harbor, New Jersey, meeting friends for lunch at the Jersey Shore. It was raining, and the restaurant was packed. We sat at the bar to wait for our table and heard the bartender ask a young lady for three forms of ID. I asked her why was that. She told me she had a Colorado Driver's License, and they thought it was fake.

"Oh," I said. "My brother Patrick just bought a house in Denver. He works at the United Airlines training center." She beckoned to an older man sitting at a table close by. "Dad," she said, "come over here; this lady has a brother who works with you at United." Her father walked over sporting his Naval Aviation shirt, and I told him my last name was Downey. He replied, "You're related to my flight instructor who trained me on the Boeing 777! He's a great guy." He then proceeded to call Pat from his cell phone. It's a small world!

New Orleans Encounter

My sister Liz and I just arrived in New Orleans and were waiting for my friend to arrive on a different plane. We put our luggage at her hotel, the Monteleone, and then went across the street to get a snack and a drink. I happened to overhear the guy at the next table state that he lived in Hollywood. A good friend of mine who introduced me to my Ron lives in Hollywood,

I took a chance and said, "I have a friend who lives in Old Hollywood." To which, he replied, "I live in the Hollywood Hills area."

I said, "My son's dad has a good friend who lives in Hollywood Hills. He edits the *TV show* Ray Donovan."

The guy put his glass down, and with widened eyes, he said, "You know my interior design client."

"Sure, I do," I said. "He went to Dartmouth with Ron, and we went to his wedding in Pasadena. We gave them a hand-carved wooden salad bowl handcrafted by my father-in-law."

"I live right near them, and that salad bowl is on their new kitchen island." He then texted his client who gave a quick confirmation.

Co-Creation Exercises

I: News Fast

This week, take a distraction fast – no news, no complaining, no gossip, no angry responses to posts on Instagram or Facebook, no horror movies, etc. Ignore those click throughs on your home page and again, do not watch the news. Really? A whole week without Trump or Biden news? Yes, you can do it!

II. Successful Life Moments

Create a page in your journal to record your successful life moments. Look back at this page often!

Then, each day this week, write in your journal about those moments in your life where everything clicked. What did it feel like? Write about the time of year it happened, the smells in the air, and anything special you can remember. How did you feel? Get into a relaxed space as you work on the goal setting exercises. The more you can do this, the more synchronicity shows up in your life.

III. Journal Page on Driving Forces

List your desires and see if you can identify the motivation or drivers behind what is it you are seeking. Once done, see if you can come up with a more positive driving force.

Desire	Driving Force	Positive Driving Force

Example:		
Make $$$ in Income	**Don't be afraid**	**Secure my future**

Love Synonyms
Adore
Go For
Fancy
Like
Affection
Adoration
Tenderness
Ardor
Dearest
Passion

Love Antonyms
Detest
Hate
Loathing
Revulsion
Disgust
Extreme Dislike

STEP THREE: LOVE

"**I**n order to love purely, we must surrender our old ways of thinking. For most of us, surrendering anything is difficult. We still think of surrender as failure, as something you do when you've lost the war. Actually, it is strong. It is a balance to our aggression." ~ Marianne Williamson[14]

To truly co-create what you want, you must move into a place of pure, unconditional **Love** for yourself and others. The word *unconditional* is bandied about a lot these days, but the true meaning of it is the release of judgment, whether of ourselves or of others. Many of us have been taught to be critical; we have learned to find fault. I certainly did. Therefore, we find fault with our lives, our decisions, our experiences, our parents, our jobs, our siblings, our income, our habits, our consumption … The list is endless.

If you remain in this place of judgment, restriction is where you are placing your focus, the power of your mind, and your **creative** center. You are **creating** judgment. The more you focus on the critical, the principle of attraction will draw exactly those experiences to yourself. It is unconscious invitation, and we all do it from time to time.

Before we examine the aspects of living in the grace of pure **Love**, this pattern, this filter on our view of life, or life pattern needs to be uplifted. We must substitute discernment for our judgment. Discernment is the process of knowing (through our Clarity exercises), what is working for us and supporting our true nature and desires. In discernment, we determine that we no longer wish to accept

---

14 Marianne Williamson, *A Return to Love: Reflections on the Principles of* A Course in Miracles (New York: HarperCollins, 1996).

or participate in a particular relationship, job, or experience. We release it easily (through our **Letting Go** process) and never enter the dark tunnel of judgment. Unfortunately, we may have learned at an early age that we are only "supposed" to **Let Go** of that which is "bad." Therefore, we believe we must be angry or judgmental to decide to move on or to release an uncomfortable experience.

How much easier our process is if we tap into our inner truth and simply make a decision. **Let Go** and stick to it. We do not need to judge ourselves, feel guilty, or judge the situation. We simply honor our power, our wisdom, have faith, and move on to the new. Judgment often provides us with contradictory inner voices. For example, Sally was in a difficult relationship. She needed a partner who is supportive, has ample time, and desires to spend time with her. Her boyfriend Tom was just the opposite. He loved to be the life of the party, out every night, and traveled often on business. It was not a surprise to learn that they were constantly fighting to get each other's needs met. Tom needed a girlfriend who was secure enough to give him ample room to socialize and meet the demands of his business. Neither was getting their needs met.

Now, before we continue this story. Note how your mind may have slipped into a place of judgment. Did you find Sally weak? Did you think Sally made a "bad" choice of partner? Did you think Tom was self-centered? In truth, none of this is your business. What is your business is the opportunity to study how your mind processed this story. Your goal should be to simply observe the information and trust that each one of these individuals in their own way is serving their own needs best. If you found yourself "reacting" to the position one of the partners had taken and judging it to be something other than human nature, you may need to look within yourself and find what it is about this story that you judge within yourself.

Sally decided to break up with Tom. It is easy from the outside for you, the reader, to know Sally will be much better off with a different partner. And we have absolute faith Sally would find such a man for herself. Sally, however, experienced and expressed judgment. She criticized herself for making the biggest mistake in choosing Tom in the first place. Why? Because she felt fear about the future and around her own self-worth. Her own critical judge within told her she made a mistake. To compound this, Tom was very upset, and Sally began to feel guilty for hurting him. So, now she had two judgments within:

- It is my fault I will be alone.
- I am a bad person for hurting Tom.

As we sit in the witness position, we can see that the truth is not present in Sally's thoughts. What we can also see is Sally's closed or narrow thinking. She is also operating in a mental space where she believes she deserves punishment. Until she lets go of these emotions and thoughts and begins to **Love** her decision, she will not achieve her desires.

The easiest way to move into a place of **love** is to journal everything for which you are thankful. Many start their day writing down three things such as:

- I am grateful I own my own business
- I love my son and our kitty
- I am thankful for this beautiful day

Instead of saying grace at a meal, I often go around the table and ask each person why they are thankful. It blesses our food and changes the energetic connection in the room.

This simple process of moving into a place of **love** changes your attitude and your vibrational frequency. The day works better if you let go of situations, people, or events that are bothering you and move into a place of **Love**. Other practices in the companion CC exercise book include prayer and sending love to a loved one in need. My friend Fiona's son was recently hospitalized so I sent a meal for them, so they didn't have to be bothered with cooking. These small acts of kindness are returned tenfold. Just keep giving out good energy and all will be okay. How great did I feel when she sent me a thank you note for the soup?

I have always valued the channeled work of Louise Hay. In her best-selling book, *You Can Heal Your Life*,[15] she shares that whatever illness you are facing is due to an issue in your life you need to deal with and process. All illness, according to her, is created out of a mental equivalent. By process, we mean learn to **Love** it, **let it Go,** and move on! For example, according to Louise, if you have an issue with your knee, you may have a fear of moving forward, and maybe it is time to change directions. She advised that if you experience a constant pain in your lower back to examine where you feel unsupported financially, emotionally,

---

15 Louise Hay, *You Can Heal Your Life* (Carlsbad, CA: Hay House, 2002).

or spiritually? Her research into Mental Equivalents goes back hundreds of years, and some of her research from the Christian Science teachings played a pivotal role in what she wrote. Her personal experiences with her clients documented her approach, and her many readers proved the metaphysics of her work.

Dr. Mona Lisa Schultz is a Neuroscientist who began to chronicle how her patient's symptoms represented what her patients were dealing with in life and began to see a pattern that tracked with the assertions of Louise Hay. In her bestselling book, *Awakening Intuition*,[16] Dr. Schultz shares many stories of how we are cause to our own effect through the patient's life experience contributing to their illness. For example, a man experienced bouts of hearing loss for which there was no medical explanation. On further examination, it only happened when there was something going on in his life he did ***not*** want to hear. Pay close attention to your body because it reveals to you that which you need to process and address.

Love Story: Releasing Karma from Past Lives

Some believe that we incarnate on this plane many times. One day, I was pondering this idea and declared to myself, *I release any issues that I may be holding from prior lifetimes.* I am not sure why I was inspired to make this pronouncement. But I did, and I went about my day.

My phone rang later that afternoon, and it was my friend Dorothy from Florida. She was upset with me.

"Do you know I haven't spoken to you since we last met in Florida? I was really angry when you left because you were talking about all of these new age ideas. Really? If I did something to you in a past life, what can I do about it now?"

"That's the whole point, Dorothy. We love each other now, and we can simply let any past conflicts go."

"Oh, okay."

Then, without missing a beat, she began to bring me up to the moment on what was happening in her life with her family.

---

16 Mona Lisa Schultz, MD, PhD, *Awakening Intuition: Using Your Mind-Body Network for Insight and Healing* (New York: Three Rivers Press, 1998).

Love Story: Seeking a Partner

Not long after 9/11, I flew to Wiesbaden, Germany, to make a presentation. Truth be told, for me, like many, it was actually a frightening time to get on a plane.

The trip, however, was lovely. My German colleague was gracious, and my first evening there, we ate dinner in an old Rathskeller in the City Hall. It was an architecturally magnificent, romantic building. I decided that night I wanted a partner who would treat me with the same respect as my colleague and take me on romantic getaways.

I chose not to spend the weekend with my colleagues but isolated myself down on the Rhine Gau in an old hotel castle to reflect. This was years before we used email on our phones or played with electronic devices for entertainment. I was alone, few people spoke English in the region, and there was only one English-speaking TV station which showed films of the Communist takeover of Czechoslovakia. It was very gloomy but I used my time constructively to concoct my vision of a perfect partner.

The list, along with some other specifics, read:

- Partner
- European Minded
- Handsome
- Attracted to Me
- Super Smart
- Successful
- Fun

It is important to note that **clarifying** my desire to be with someone Euro-minded meant I was ruling out the typical guy from Philadelphia. I declared that I wanted someone who was worldly, adventurous, and open to other cultures. As I will share later, I met Ron, my first husband, two months after this trip. I learned immediately he was fluent in German and lived in Berlin during college. This helped me to know immediately because of my **clarity** in preparing my "list," he was a potential partner for me.

Love Story: Replacing My Audi

Years after owning my first Audi, I purchased another pre-owned Audi, an All-Road wagon. I absolutely loved that car. Unfortunately, even though I'd purchased an extended warranty, the $4,000 in maintenance it required when I took it in for service was not covered under the warranty insurance. I was financially underwater on this car and investing any more money did not make sense. When the service department broke the news, the other person in the waiting room declared, "Looks to me like you are getting a new car!" Because my brother still worked for a Toyota dealership, I decided to switch, and I settled on a Toyota Highlander. I felt I was being practical; however, like when I bought the Saturn, my concern was that I was making the wrong decision. I called the General Manager, and he asked me what I was driving. I said wistfully, "I have a beautiful Audi All-Road that is iridescent black with chrome accents." He said, "I have just the car for you!" I drove right over and purchased the best-looking Highlander you have ever seen with chrome accents and a chrome running board and a roof rack for my Thule. I knew the car was for me, the minute I laid eyes on it because it reminded me of the All-Road. It's both luxurious and practical.

Love Exercises:

I. Bucket List

The current label for writing a list of everything you want to do, see, and feel before you leave the earth is a Bucket List (before you kick the bucket). What is on your Bucket List?

Journal Page on Bucket List

What are the important elements in your life?
What would you like to add into your life?
What in your life needs to be modified or let go of?
Where do you want to travel?
Do you want children?
What does your future look like?
How is your workday structured?
Are you in partnership?
Are you happy? Why?

How much money do you wish to make?
Is there something you wish to accomplish?
Where would you like to live?
Is there a concert you wish to see? A play?

These answers will help you make clearer decisions. For example, when my niece Melissa announced, she was getting married in the Canadian Rockies at the Banff Springs Hotel (Fairmont), I knew immediately I would make the trip because Banff and Lake Louise were on my Bucket List. My good friend knew she was going to the World Series when the Phillies won the National League Pennant is another example. That event, along with going in person to *Saturday Night Live*, is on her list, so she found a way for that to happen.

II. Gratitude Journal

Every morning, before you get out of bed, or while you are taking a shower, remember what you are grateful for. We also always state our gratitude before every meal. This practice helps us shift to a place of positivity much more easily than we might have employed in the past.

III. Write a Love Letter to Yourself

As my yoga teacher Heather likes to say, "Look in the mirror and say something nice to yourself!"

Take the time to sit down and write yourself a letter, as if you were your own parent. Highlight all of the generous and giving things you do for your friends, family, and even strangers. When you are having a moment of doubt or a slip in your faith, read the letter to yourself; it changes your outlook. Here are some of the highlights from a sample letter:

- Suzanne gives a lot of money to charity to support those who are hungry and in need of medical care.
- Suzanne gives back to her community.
- Suzanne is lots of fun.

- Suzanne works hard to remain positive and surrender to her perfect life.
- Suzanne takes the time to take care of herself with exercise, therapy, and yoga.

Feel free to borrow any of these!

Letting Go Synonyms
Release
Liberate
Free
Discharge
Circulate
Distribute

Letting Go Antonyms
Grip
Grasp
Clasp
Clutch
Clamp
Clench

STEP FOUR: LETTING GO

Quote from Buddha on the definition of a Good Life:

> "How much you loved . . .
> How gently you lived . . .
> And how gracefully you let go of things not meant for you."

The **Letting Go** Practice of the **Clarity** Model encompasses many healing aspects which support you in releasing your past worries, regrets, anger, hurts, grievances, wrongs, and misgivings.

The concept is amazingly simple:

Holding on to past pain only keeps you in the past!

Your brain does not understand that something happened a year ago or 30 years ago. If you keep revisiting a painful memory, you experience it over and over and over. Not only is this not healthy, but it also keeps you from moving forward and making room for new, positive outcomes. More importantly, you may not be aware you may be revisiting the memory in your subconscious mind. This is why trauma counseling and hypnotherapy are so effective; they retrain your memories, so they don't trigger as much stress. I have had tremendous stress relief working with a therapist trained in Eye Movement Desensitization and Reprocessing (EMDR) therapy.

Become a Magnet for Healthy Opportunities

To move forward, you not only need to **let go** of your regrets and grievances, but you also need to forgive those who may have caused the pain in the first place. In his book, *Forgive for Good*, Dr. Fred Luskin compares holding on to your upset with someone to *renting them a room in your head*. His research shows that forgiveness benefits the person doing the forgiving. It does not release the bad actor from their actions; forgiveness simply frees up your brain to accept new, positive possibilities.

> "Forgiveness has been shown to reduce anger, hurt, depression and stress and lead to greater feelings of optimism, hope, compassion and self-confidence . . . Forgiveness is above all a choice. It is a choice to find peace and live life fully. We can choose either to remain stuck in the pain and frustration of the past or to move on to the potential of the future. It is a choice we can all make and it is a choice that will lead us to a healthier and happier life."[17]

There is a saying in the New Thought movement that "the universe abhors a vacuum." So, when you clean house, mentally, emotionally, physically, and spiritually, you are making way for the new to come in. My former husband and I were unable to conceive until he removed all vestiges of his first marriage from our house. (Well, he did hold on to his Joseph Abboud tuxedo, but when we started parenting counseling, he ultimately **let that go,** too.)

Here is a list of the many things that you can **let go** of:

- Anger
- Resentment
- Comparing ourselves to others
- Things you are not using
- Clothing that does not fit
- Items that bring unpleasant memories
- Clutter
- Paper Files
- Negative Relationships
- Toxic Situations
- Fear
- Falsehoods that others may say about you

---

17 Dr. Fred Luskin, *Forgive for Good: A Proven Prescription for Health and Happiness* (New York: Harper Collins, 2002), 217.

You should absolutely apply this principle when traveling. My colleague John asked me what I would do if my flight were canceled in Paris. John had this happen to him and he was given the option to wait for new equipment or take the same flight the next day. I quickly advised him that I would immediately grab a hotel room and take another day in Paris. "That's funny," he said, "We decided to wait it out. It was a seemingly endless day, and they did not call the official cancellation of the flight until midnight. We slept (or tried to sleep) in the airport, and the new flight finally left at 10:00 the following morning. The other flight I could have taken left at the same time the next day and we were all in international arrivals in Philadelphia at the same time." John wasted an entire day in the airport.

As I wrote part of this section, I was trapped in a nine-person passenger van for an endless ride back to Vienna. I worked hard to **go with the flow** by taking a nap, making sure I didn't drink too much water, necessitating a bathroom stop, and enjoying the time with my son. At the same time, I was delighted when we pulled into our hotel area and terminated the trip. We drove over 13 hours in blizzard conditions on this short seven-day journey. The best thing for me to do in this moment was to avoid looking at the clock! I also worked on the **Love** step of the model by being thankful that I wasn't the one driving the vehicle in that crazy weather.

I also used the trip to Austria as a template for my recent trip to Banff. After examining what I was anxious about, I then found a solution. For example, I booked a hotel room on the club floor at the airport, sparing no expense, so we would be fed and on time for our 6:00 a.m. flight to Calgary.

Suffering is a choice, but unpleasant and unexpected events do not always have to trigger suffering. The best way to **create** a happy and carefree life is to "go with the flow." It is best to embrace the delays, setbacks, and the people around you. There are many stories of unexpected delays through traffic or illness that kept people from being in the World Trade Center on 9/11, and they were miraculously saved from the destruction. Sometimes, a delay is helping to protect you. If you can keep a positive attitude, positive events continually occur in your life. God's delays are not God's denials!

The philosophical premise of the New Thought is that our thought processes contribute to what appears in our life. Thus, if your thoughts are negative, doubtful, and distrustful, you create people and events to support these descriptions. Your life will be fraught with difficulty, mistrust, and lack of ease. Again, this is a demonstration of unconscious invitation Ernest Holmes speaks to in the Science of Mind. The sooner you recognize your own personal power, and **let go** of the past, the sooner you can get your life and your career on the track you choose. As I say, if you tell the world that your life is difficult, Spirit replies, "Why, yes, it is!" So, try it out. Start to tell yourself every day that your life is working beautifully, and everything is in perfect order and harmony.

Sometimes, incidents occur to turn your course in life. Instead of resisting them, embrace them as opportunities for change. And, of course, **let go** of whatever is in your way. This is how you can begin to live in the divine flow of life.

Let's start at the beginning: Clear your mind of negative patterns. Train your brain to act with laser-like precision to select your choices in life.

Ask yourself what you need to **let go** of and then journal the answers you receive.

Another way of understanding the **Letting Go** step of the **Clarity** model is to think of a garden hose with a kink in it. Negative emotions are the "kinks" that stop the flow of good into your life. In releasing anger, trauma memory, resentment, and other upsetting emotions, you open to happiness and fulfillment. I highly recommend eye movement therapy (EMDR) work for releasing trauma memories, whether emotional or physical because it serves to rewire the brain to remodel or shift a past experience from painful or triggering to an opportunity for change. I no longer react; I respond because the past has no authority over the present.

Anger is a way of covering up hurt feelings, and it changes nothing in the physical reality; it is only a catalyst for change. My approach is this. Root out the seven deadly Christian sins from your life:

- Pride
- Greed
- Wrath
- Envy
- Lust

- Gluttony
- Sloth

Once you do, you will be well along the path toward creating a more positive life.

Let Go of Scarcity Thinking

Scarcity thinking is the belief in a restricted universe. Edwene Gaines, the prosperity Guru, says there is enough to go around for every man, woman, and child on the earth. It is the *belief* that there is not enough to go around that gets us into trouble through lack thinking.

- Not enough money
- Not enough love
- Not enough friends
- Not enough jobs

The list is endless. Pay attention to your thoughts. This is why envy is a deadly sin. It is the ultimate form of thinking that if someone receives something good, then you cannot generate the same form of abundance. Journal about the ways you think the Universe is limited, or if you share your wealth and advice, you will have less. The opposite is true. The more you give and share, then the more your good flows to you. Maya Angelou said, "First you learn, then you teach; first you give, then you receive."

There are many ways to **let go** of past negativity and old belief systems that may have been instilled in you as a child: Psychotherapy, Art Therapy, Meditation, Hypnosis, Self-reflection, Prayer, Yoga, Dance, Massage, Reiki Energy Healing, Acupuncture, Scream Therapy, Labyrinth walking, etc. The list is endless. We call this Core Belief work. Most of your core beliefs were instilled in childhood, and you may not realize the "operating system" that is running in the background of the computer of your brain. For example, when I was born, my parents were well-to-do and made a lot of money. All my clothes came from posh department stores, and we lived at the beach. Circumstances changed when we moved to Pennsylvania, and my dad stopped working. My mother, raising five children, went to go to work full-time. Even with relatively no money, we lived in an affluent neighborhood. There were years when a family member helped pay the property taxes, or we would have lost the house. Unfortunately, my parents did not shield me from this harsh reality, so I grew up thinking there is never enough money. However, I also grew up seeing my friends' parents prospering and other people making a lot of money. So, I learned to balance the two schools of thought. The Science of Mind has helped me to take action to overcome my fear around money, and I have been financially successful in my adult life. Recently, through divorce, I was required to pay my husband a significant sum of money, and I did as instructed. Now, I am simply moving on by formulating a plan to make the money back.

Make Room for the New!

Once you have set your goals, it is time to conduct a congruency test. Are your goals in alignment with your actions? Where in your life do you need to make changes to allow room for the new? Remember, a garden needs fresh tilled soil before you can plant new seeds.

**Be BRAVE - you deserve the GREAT results
this work will bring to you, your company, and your profits.**

The congruency test can be difficult. It requires a frank, honest overview of your life. This is why coaches are so popular these days: No one wants to go it alone under this scrutiny!

1. Take some time to complete your goal setting, by category and priority.
2. Take a good look at what you need to change in your life.
3. Work on the Letting Go Exercises over the next few weeks.

This process will tell you where you may be engaging in self-sabotage, where you are afraid and most importantly where you have DOUBT about your goals. If you don't believe in your vision, it is MUCH less likely to come true! Working on the Letting Go exercises will open your life up to more goodness and happiness. It's said that the Universe abhors a vacuum and will work to fill it with your clear intentions.

My Letting Go Poem on Forgiveness
How insidious this rooted weed
That has festered in my being.
Germinated so long ago.
Like a dandelion, this resistance
To release and let go of past deeds.
Regrows stronger after many cuttings.
Until finally, I dislodge the root.
This underground growth can be tenacious.
And perhaps I have grown accustomed, even comfortable.
With the earth it holds
Where will I be with open space?
I claim my right to a tended heart.
For my destiny depends upon it
I bravely embrace the images of those from whom.
I have claimed pain and boldly turn the plough
In letting go, I know my ultimate love for myself.

Letting Go Story: Have Spirit Solve Your Problems (The Box)

Years ago, I offered to help my friend Betsey pack her things for her big move to Arizona. She appeared upset about the move and showed it by criticizing my packing skills. In the packing process, I experienced a horrific allergy attack. I was definitely reacting to the situation, along with the loads of dust and cat hair that accumulated in her apartment. As I was leaving her apartment, she gave me a large box containing partyware such as paper plates and forks, etc. I took it, albeit reluctantly, as I noticed cat hair all over it. I put it in the trunk of my car; I dared not open it because of the allergens. I was upset with myself for even accepting it.

A few days later, Betsey called me and told me that her friends were throwing her a going-away party, and she would like me to come early and bring the box she'd given me. I was irritated by her request and wished I'd said "*no*" because the time of the party interfered with a planned trip to the beach. I wondered how I would resolve the situation and decided not to think about it by surrendering the solution to Spirit

Two days later, I was called to New York on a business trip. On the drive home, I stopped at a rest area 65 miles north of my home to get some coffee and a snack. I was waiting in the Cinnabon coffee line, and for some reason, I turned around to look behind me. There stood my friend Betsey. She drove up to New York to visit her ailing grandmother and like me, she was on her way home. I told her I still had the box in my car, and we walked together outside. I returned the box to her in the middle of the New Jersey Turnpike parking lot a long way from home. How auspicious! My problem was resolved. I surrendered the outcome and trusted in Spirit. Smile. . . It's in moments like these that it is clear there is order in the Universe.

Letting Go: How Anger Attracts Negativity

Driving to New York on the New Jersey Turnpike, I was feeling angry while mulling over a difficult family situation. My attention to my driving was not the best in that moment as I was watching a tow truck that was hauling unmarked police cruisers. Suddenly, I saw the tow truck coming into my lane. I heard a voice say, *Just slow down; you will be okay.* I was pushed into the cement barrier a few times but was able to drive the car and walked away from the accident only in need of massage and chiropractic. Upon reflection, I realized my anger and inattention created this nasty experience. Unconscious invitation rears its head again! At the same time, I was guided on how to survive the accident and blessed by two good Samaritans who stopped to help me.

Another time, while driving, again, I was feeling angry at someone I was seeing because he was not pursuing our relationship the way I wanted. He lived in a different part of the country and long-distance relationships are rarely easy. Another car came too close for comfort, and it triggered the memory of the first accident, and I accidently jerked the wheel so hard I did a complete 360-degree turn on the Garden State Parkway. I ended up safely parked on the shoulder. At that moment, I knew I needed to let the anger go and move on from this relationship.

A driver pulled up on the shoulder behind me. She walked up and knocked on my window. I told her, "I'm fine, I don't need any help." And she said, "I know, I can tell; it's a miracle you did not hit another car. I just wanted to see who the magician was who was driving this car."

Letting Go Exercises:

I. **Create a Journal about what you *have* let go of and what you would *like* to let go of.**

Much of this exercise will have to do with relationships that are no longer serving you. It could be the passing of close friends or family. This could be old or forgotten friendships, a failed investment, an opportunity you did not take, etc. This list is endless, too!

II. **Letting Go Exercise: Anger Expression**

You have your unique relationship with anger. To begin, answer the following questions:

1. Is there something I am angry about?
2. Is it a past or present hurt?
3. Does my present experience feel familiar? Have I experienced this before?
4. What do I feel I lost in the process?
5. What is it I am trying to reclaim?

You may wish to complete this exercise a few times to address specific issues. Do not be fearful of feeling your anger. Feel it! Feel how powerful you are! And when you are completely in touch with your emotions, you are going to express them. Speak the words out loud to dissipate their negative energy so it doesn't reside in the physical body and show up as illness/disease. This work is not about right or wrong behavior. It is about how you feel. You have a right to your feelings. As you move in consciousness, the likelihood of these feelings getting triggered diminishes. You will eventually be skilled at not taking things personally. The point of anger work is to connect with your pure power and reclaim your boundaries. No one needs to be hurt to move through this process. In fact, that would only continue the stream of anger. Eckhart Tolle says never say I am angry. Say I feel angry, then investigate it. You have many choices on how to express anger, and you may create your own:

1. Write a letter (that you may not mail) to someone you feel has hurt you.
2. Write a letter to yourself to reclaim that which you feel you have lost.
3. Take a walk in the ocean, jump in a pool, or sit in a hot bath to cleanse these feelings.
4. Find a pillow and a soft bat and smash your anger away.
5. Have a loving, centered conversation with the person you have issues with. Allow them to speak without interruption.
6. Write all of your feelings down on paper and build a big fire to burn what you've written and are now able to release.
7. Perform a ritual of hand and feet washing to cleanse these feelings.
8. Go outside with some chalk and draw a big box on the driveway. Step in inside and announce that you are safe and protected in this space. Symbolically leave your anger outside the box.
9. Sit in nature for some time and visualize the anger floating up to the sky.
10. Put together some things in a box that remind you of the person you are releasing and take them to a sacred place and bury the box. It is also great to remove objects and photographs from your home or office that provide a constant reminder of the person.

III. **Letting Go Exercise: Listen daily to the Beatles' *"Let It Be"* or the theme song from *Frozen* "*Let It Go"***

IV. **Letting Go Exercise: Make a list of the activities that put you in a good mood. That way, you will have tools prepared to Let Go of a bad mood such as:**

   a. Reading
   b. Talking with a Friend
   c. Yoga
   d. Swimming

Embody Synonyms
Exemplify
Symbolize
Represent
Personify
Characterize
Represent
Incarnate
Epitomize

Anthropomorphize
Humanize
Bring to Life
Breathe life into

Embody Antonyms
Disembody
Death

STEP FIVE: EMBODY

"There is one way to avoid criticism: Do nothing, say nothing, and be nothing."

—Aristotle

Some believe you can just state your affirmations and the situations and your desires come your way. This is not entirely true! You must also take action and move in the direction of your dreams. In New Thought, this is generally known as *Treat and Move Your Feet*. That is, we not only pray and create affirmations about our desires but take physical action toward letting things happen.

A very famous sales teacher, Tom Hopkins, shared that growing up, he was "dirt" poor. He made a conscious decision to be a rich man when he grew up. Not only did he set his goals and believe that he could create significant wealth, he also looked for a way to experience being wealthy beyond measure. He visualized traveling around the world because that is what rich people do. And to **embody** this goal and bring his dream into the physical realm, Tom went to the international airport and watched all the rich travelers embarking on their flights and disembarking from their journeys. This is the essence of embodiment. It was his unique way of removing scarcity thinking from his memories, changing his mindset, and his life.

This is evident in a weight loss plan. Remember, losing weight is not a goal; it is a process. The goal is to be fit and healthy. Weight loss is all about your metabolism and the total calories ingested proportionately to total calories burned. More importantly, it's about controlling your emotional responses, which I will discuss shortly. These days we say, "Get your steps in" to make sure you are burning calories and boosting your metabolism. Walking 1,000 steps a day is the perfect example of **embodiment**.

Hunger creates change. Get in touch with what you are hungry for and then work to find examples of those who have achieved what you desire. Learn the steps they followed to find their success. A great study on success, Malcolm Gladwell's *Outliers*[18] witnesses that the great success stories began with embodiment. Practice, practice, practice! He shares that Tiger Woods began hitting golf balls as a three-year-old. The same premise was used with the tennis stars Serena and Venus Williams with tennis rackets. Set your sights on what it is you desire and begin to see it happening in your mind's eye. The first step is believing your success is possible. The second step is making a firm decision to move forward on that goal. The third step is to take action while continually monitoring your thoughts; it is essential that you focus on the positive possibilities in your life and accept reality for what it is, instead of fighting what has appeared in your life. Believe me, I get it, I have had two friends and my first husband betray me. But I am clear that if I don't **Let Go,** my future happiness will be threatened.

Daniel Goleman introduced the concept of *Emotional Intelligence* [19] in his bestselling book of the same name. An effective leader has a great degree of understanding of human behavior and uses this thinking in his own life. This translates into the ability to communicate clearly, to regulate his/her responses to a perceived threat, and to maintain strength and focus in a crisis response. In short, an emotionally intelligent manager is knowledgeable about the very natural human fight/flight response and makes sure his/her rational and cognitive brain functions are engaged before he acts or responds to something uncomfortable or threatening. The key is understanding that trauma emotions are stored in the amygdala region of the brain known as the reptilian brain because it only knows how to fight for survival. This portion of the brain can take over your entire response to any perceived threat.

---

18 Malcom Gladwell, *Outliers: The Story of Success* (New York: Little, Brown and Company, 2008).

19 Daniel Goleman, *Emotional Intelligence*: Why It Can Matter More Than IQ (New York: Bantam Books, 2005).

Let's review the specific aspects of the fight/flight response, also known as the sympathetic nervous system:

- Something happens in your life that makes you uncomfortable and ties to a conscious or subconscious trauma memory.
- Your brain perceives you are under attack and moves into survival mode.
- This triggers the release of a hormone, which in turn tells the adrenal glands to release cortisol.
- Cortisol makes all kinds of things happen in your body to increase glucose to give you extra strength to outrun a charging bull.
- This causes your insulin levels to rise, which elevates your heartbeat and shuts down other bodily functions including digestion.
- Your breathing becomes shallow so you can take in more oxygen.
- This fuel release allows super strength, which allows, for instance, a mom to lift a car off of her child in an emergency.

This physiological response sounds great if you need to make a run for it. If you don't engage in physical activity, you will have an abundance of insulin, glucose, fatty acids, and neuropeptides generated in your body with no immediate physical release. This can greatly contribute to disease if you sustain these levels due to repeated stresses. It is for this reason that exercise and mindfulness are so important to sustaining a healthy body. It is also why calming techniques activate the parasympathetic nervous system and are important for your health. Because of the bad car accident I experienced years ago, to this day, if I see a car coming at me on the right side at a particular angle, it triggers the fight/flight response. My brain thinks the truck is going to hit me again. When that happens, I take a few deep breaths and remind myself the accident happened years ago and is not my reality today.

Our perception triggers this response to both imagined and real dangers. This physical response does not assist you unless the fear is real; in fact, it very often makes your mind go blank. Have you ever had your mind go blank during a public presentation or some other perceived stress?

When the brain believes it perceives such an event, the conscious mind is bypassed, and the amygdala instructs the body to prepare for a fight. This means, in effect, the brain has two memory systems - one for ordinary facts and one for emotionally charged ones.

We only need our current reality to mirror a small part of old trauma, and the crisis response is triggered. The more traumas you have experienced, the easier to trigger a fight/flight response. When this response is activated, we are operating from a more primitive part of our brain. Who knows what your original trauma was? It could be feeling embarrassment at show and tell in the first grade or fear taught by our parents.

The research shows that whether it is a present-day event or a memory, it is now irrelevant. This amygdala arousal creates difficulty for you when there is no threat. In the case of stress arousal, there is no use or release for this increased physical capacity, and we must learn to "turn off" the mechanism through relaxation techniques.

How do you stop your fight/flight stress response? There are more mindfulness practices in many of the **Clarity Concepts**™ exercises, but here are a few ideas that are now labeled as *mindfulness* or *minding your mind*:

- Pause before you respond when under stress
- Focus on your breath
- Breathe deeply and calmly
- Stretch gently
- Take a break and sit quietly to empty your mind so no stress is present
- Wash your hands to break the energy cycle

The best way to control your mind and body is through meditation. There is new research on how effective meditation is at supporting recovery from addiction, healing an illness, and creating happiness. In his book *10% Happier*, well-known newscaster, Dan Harris claims that meditation "tamed the voice in his head, reduced his stress . . . and [he] found self-help that actually works."[20] Dan advises that his biggest impediment to adopting a meditation practice was the stigma associated with mindfulness practices.

---

20 Dan Harris, *10% Happier: How I Tamed the Voice in My Head, Reduced Stress Without Losing My Edge, and Found Self-Help That Actually Works—A True Story* (New York: Harper Collins, 2019).

"It was mildly embarrassing to admit to most people that I meditated. This was largely because the practice was popularized in this country by Beat poets, robed gurus, and hippies, and that cultural hangover persisted. Stylistically, the presentation of the average meditation struck me as a bizarre cousin of the stentorian, monotone that TV reporters employ … Buddhist teachers had their own set." ~ Dan Harris

One embodiment exercise I practice daily happens before I get out of bed. I visualize a body of water to clear my mind before I start my day. I also took the advice of my hypnotherapist and changed my cell phone to a song much less jarring than the alarm I had been using for years. It makes me smile when I wake up. I also employ three weekly commitments:

1. Pilates or Yoga: Pilates helps me to avoid back pain, and the physical and breathing exercises themselves are counterintuitive and force me to get out of my head and into my body. The minute we can get out of our reactive mind, we have a great degree of control over our emotions and our lives as was documented in the research at Emory University on Meditation.

2. Power of Eight Meditation[21] This is a meditation process centered on intentions created by journalist Lynne McTaggart practiced when we meet weekly as a group on Zoom. The process is simple:

   1. Set the time aside.
   2. Each person sets an intention.
   3. Call in Spirit and create sacred space.
   4. Our guide chooses a "receiver," although, all receive the energy.
   5. There isa guided mediation in which tremendous universal energy is shared.
   6. We share our experience on the journey. It's remarkable how many of us will have the same experiences and vision. No journey is the same.
   7. We close the session.

3. Zoom Personal Training with Jackie Carroll. I met Jackie during Covid and

21 Lynne McTaggart, *The Power of Eight: Harnessing the Miraculous Energies of a Small Group to Heal Others, Your Life, and the World* (New York: Atria/Simon& Shuster, 2017).

continue to work with her remotely on Zoom every Tuesday morning. She is uplifting and kicks my butt. She closes every session with the saying:

> *I give thanks*
> *for this body,*
> *for this breath, and*
> ***for its ability to change,***
> *Namaste*
> Jackie Carroll

Part of letting go is *paying it forward* in accordance with the law of circulation. Holding onto money can cause problems in your life. In the same way, withholding affection, the truth, or one's time can stop the flow. More abundance comes to you as you support the people, places and institutions with whom and where you are spiritually fed. Give to your church, your spiritual center, your friends, your college, my friend Joe Ogilvie's Rail Trail preservation and restoration in New Lebanon, NY (look up Corkscrew Rail Trail on Facebook), those in need, and the issues that you support. These gifts will return to you multiplied.

Embodiment: The *Wear Sunscreen* proposed commencement speech by Mary Schmich[22]

Ladies and gentlemen of the class of '97:

Wear Sunscreen

If I could offer you only one tip for the future, sunscreen would be it. The long-term benefits of sunscreen have been proved by scientists, whereas the rest of my advice has no basis more reliable than my own meandering experience. I will dispense this advice now

Enjoy the power and beauty of your youth. Oh, never mind. You will not understand the power and beauty of your youth until they've faded. But trust me, in 20 years, you'll look back at photos of yourself and recall in a way you can't grasp now how much possibility lay before you and how fabulous you really looked. You are not as fat as you imagine.

---

22 Mary Schmich, June 1, 1997, Chicago Tribune, Tribune Publishing, IL

Don't worry about the future. Or worry, but know that worry is as effective as trying to solve an algebra equation by chewing bubble gum. The real troubles in your life are apt to be things that never crossed your worried mind. The kind that blindsides you at 4 p.m. on some idle Tuesday.

Do one thing every day that scares you.

Sing.

Don't be reckless with other people's hearts. Don't put up with people who are reckless with yours.

Floss.

Don't waste your time on jealousy. Sometimes you're ahead; sometimes you're behind. The race is long, and in the end, it's only with yourself.

Remember compliments you receive. Forget the insults. If you succeed in doing this, tell me how.

Keep your old love letters. Throw away your old bank statements.

Stretch.

Don't feel guilty if you don't know what you want to do with your life. The most interesting people I know didn't know at 22 what they wanted to do with their lives. Some of the most interesting 40-year-olds I know still don't.

Get plenty of calcium. Be kind to your knees. You'll miss them when they're gone.

Maybe you'll marry, maybe you won't. Maybe you'll have children, maybe you won't. Maybe you'll divorce at 40, maybe you'll dance the funky chicken on your 75th wedding anniversary. Whatever you do, don't congratulate yourself too much, or berate yourself either. Your choices are half chance. So are everybody else's.

Enjoy your body. Use it every way you can. Don't be afraid of it or of what other people think of it. It's the greatest instrument you'll ever own.

Dance, even if you have nowhere to do it but your living room.

Read the directions, even if you don't follow them.

Do not read beauty magazines. They will only make you feel ugly.

Get to know your parents. You never know when they'll be gone for good. Be nice to your siblings. They're your best link to your past and the people most likely to stick with you in the future.

Understand that friends come and go, but with a precious few you should hold on. Work hard to bridge the gaps in geography and lifestyle, because the older you get, the more you need the people who knew you when you were young.

Live in New York City once, but leave before it makes you hard. Live in Northern California once, but leave before it makes you soft.

Accept certain inalienable truths: Prices will rise. Politicians will philander. You, too, will get old. And when you do, you'll fantasize that when you were young, prices were reasonable, politicians were noble and children respected their elders.

Respect your elders.

Don't expect anyone else to support you. Maybe you have a trust fund. Maybe you'll have a wealthy spouse. But you never know when either one might run out.

Don't mess too much with your hair, or by the time you're 40, it will look 85.

Be careful whose advice you buy but be patient with those who supply it. Advice is a form of nostalgia. Dispensing it is a way of fishing the past from the disposal, wiping it off, painting over the ugly parts and recycling it for more than it's worth.

But trust me on the sunscreen.

—Mary Schmich

Embodiment Story: The Power of Eight by Lynne McTaggart

After I joined the Power of Eight Group, I watched my business blossom and grow. In one session, I set an intention for prosperity, and we discussed that we never know where our business, prosperity, income, or wealth is going to come from. One day, the phone rang, and it was an old friend who was a former client. He told me he needed insurance help with a new startup and immediately paid me $50,000! A few years later, I made a large emotional donation to the Philadelphia Children's Alliance, and not one week later, I was awarded a project that has easily made up for that charitable donation. Recently, someone approached me about resurfacing my driveway, something I have been wanting to do. The asphalt company salesman convinced me I would save over $3,000 if I did it when he was paving another property nearby. It's odd that I trusted someone who randomly knocked on my door, but he promised me I would pay no money until it was complete. The price was $7,000. I agreed, and he did a phenomenal job! I paid him via check when he finished, and the next day, I booked a new project with a retainer of $7,000. Tosha Silver's book, *It's Not Your Money: How to Live Fully from Divine Abundance*, has many examples of the law of circulation.[23]

Embodiment Story: Children

When I met my husband, he asked me on our first date if I wanted to have children. I told him I was not sure about having kids, but if I married a blond, I might have to "*shoot the gene pool.*" Meaning, I would most likely then have a child with blond hair, even though my hair is dark blond. Well, I later found out his hair was blond and had changed color since childhood. We now have a beautiful son with blond hair. Coincidence? It's hard to believe Mackie is now 16 and thriving. He is a wonderful son who is loving and mature and most importantly, a very hard worker.

Embodiment Story: The Beach House

I love being at the beach. Sometimes I wonder if it comes from the days when I was three years old and we lived three houses from the Long Island Sound in Port Washington, New York. While my uncle has a beautiful oceanfront beach house in New Jersey, we have a large family, so it was often very crowded. For this reason, I wanted my own house at the shore.

---

23 Tosha Silver, *It's Not Your Money: How to Live Fully from Divine Abundance* (Carlsbad, CA: Hay House, 2020).

At the time, my neighbors just purchased a lovely condominium in Brigantine, New Jersey. I really like the commute from our home to the beach where they lived. About a year later, I began to look at houses. At the time, I did not have the money for a down payment, but I was certain the money would come to us.

My husband did not like the houses we looked at in Brigantine. He just kept saying, "No, No, No, we do not need a beach house." As money came in, I began to put it aside for some of the down payment.

In August of 2009, my friend and I were scheduled to drive that weekend to my uncle's beach house with my son and stepdaughters. The day before we left, I received word that my friend's niece died from a heroin overdose in Atlantic City. I attended the funeral and sent the kids ahead with my friend.

The funeral was held in the Catholic Church I attended as a child. It was comforting and familiar to be there even though, I had not been in the church for over 30 years. It looked EXACTLY the same. As I sat through the service, I received a message from Spirit, *You do not want a beach house near Atlantic City. Strange,* I thought, as both my husband and my friend were dead set against a house in Brigantine. My friend wanted me to look in the town of North Wildwood in Cape May County, New Jersey, because she had tons of family there. Sitting in church, I thought *Okay, let's check out North Wildwood.* Friends of mine lived on the island and in Avalon, the next island over, as I spent many college and post-college summer weekends there.

The following weekend, I met with my realtor and looked at houses in North Wildwood. I liked the island, the trees, the activities, and the houses available. A large house was preferred so that I never had to turn anyone away. My husband wanted a condominium so we would not have maintenance, lawn care, etc. He also wanted a house that would appeal to renters as he did not want to be a "weekend warrior" slogging through traffic every weekend to get to the beach.

I didn't find a house I liked that weekend, but I sent my Ron down the following weekend. Much to my surprise, he loved North Wildwood! As his college friend said, "Of course, he loved it with the island's Doo Wop history." It turns out that the island was the major New Jersey Shore music destination until the casinos opened in Atlantic City.

I was still pulling the money together for a shore house down payment and was beginning to worry that I couldn't buy what I wanted. My husband cautiously looked at our mortgage, income, and rental income projections. During this time, my mother called and said she would lend us $30,000 to buy the house, and the loan had no repayment period on it. We were set; we just had to find a house.

While I was travelling on business in San Francisco, Ron sent me a video of two available townhouses in North Wildwood. We agreed on the one on 20th Street as the best buy. Coincidentally, I had already picked out a pre-construction home on 20th. The reason we did not pursue it is because it was not a condominium. That house is on my block.

Our home has been wonderful for the family. Rental interest on the property is high as it is a quick walk to the amusement pier. And some of the homes that suffered construction delays during the recession have been completed and fixed up. Most importantly, it turned out to be a fantastic investment!

Embodiment Story: How I Started and Maintain My Consulting Business

After I asked the Universe for a new job, I took a job with an engineering firm that hired me to start a Risk Management consulting practice. I was concerned from the start, that the friend who introduced me, was given a partnership and the same offer had not been made to me. I addressed that issue on my first day on the job. I was told that I did not have a non-compete and could take any business that I sold into a new job. Before I had left my old job at West Pharam, I was offered a job with SCHOTT Corporation, a glass manufacturer. I turned it down because I did not want to relocate back to the NY metro area. Instead, I sent SCHOTT a Risk Consulting Proposal from my new firm. As my discomfort with the new job grew, I decided to take action.

I called up General Counsel at SCHOTT and asked him if I could propose risk consulting for them from my own firm. He replied, *Of course, I don't know these people*. So, I left and started my own firm with only a four-month contract. I announced to a colleague at Penn State University Great Valley that I was leaving my job and he said, *Great, I need you to teach my two classes because I have resigned also*. When I told him I wanted to be a motivational speaker someday, he had suggested that I become a professor to get public speaking practice. The next thing I knew I was teaching 14 hours a week in an intensive class in Crisis Management, and I have been a teacher, mentor, and coach ever since.

When the contract expired, I negotiated the hardest deal, because I knew it would set the tone for the future. I am still working with this client; it's been 26 years since I made the brave decision to start out on my own. It's important to tend to your business and have support groups, do networking, and create sales opportunities. The true essence of embodiment is meeting people, sharing your value proposition, and having repeat business come to you. Don't be shy!

Embodiment Exercises:

I. Take Care of your Body

Set a goal to improve your health and find a yoga teacher, a gym, or a doctor to support you.

The goals are unlimited. Here are some ideas:

1. Be fit and healthy.
2. Reduce coffee intake.
3. Take vitamins.
4. Take frequent breaks to reduce stress when working.
5. Get outside in nature.
6. Quit a bad habit.

Be gentle with yourself. Research on change says it's more likely to stick if you take it slowly and gently in small, single steps.

II. Move your future forward by making a list of steps you can take to reach your goals

1. Take risks.
2. Keep affirming your new potential.
3. Meet new people.
4. Find yourself a mentor or mentoring group.
5. Build your LinkedIn page.
6. Join a networking or industry group.

7. Get a degree or a certificate to further your career (continuing education).

8. Manage upward by learning your boss' communication style preference.

9. Have a clear set path for your career.

10. Quit a job that you don't like.

11. Take on more responsibility at work.

12. Don't be afraid to self-promote.

13. Take a job that's a little outside your current scope and push yourself.

14. If you are a female, find a passion - coworkers relate more to women with a cause (I know it may seem odd).

15. Be a lifelong learner.

16. Read the books that I have footnoted in this manuscript.

17. Make sure you do something you love every day. It could be as simple as calling your mother.

18. Watch some TED talks.

19. Listen to motivational speakers.

20. Develop and follow your intuition.

III. **Take action on some of the Career Embodiment Practices from Leadership Professor Elaine Mercier**

1. Know your value, know your worth; specifically, know the compensation market rate for your position or the position you're interested in.

2. Be prepared to negotiate salary/benefits/bonuses, etc.

3. Keep your resume current/updated.

4. Don't be afraid to make a lateral move that offers learning and personal development opportunities

5. Follow the advice of Eleanor Roosevelt, "Everyday, do one thing that scares you!"

6. Take care of yourself and practice radical self-care.

7. Make time at the end of each workweek to reflect on what has occurred. How does it impact future actions and strategies?

8. Practice self-awareness and demonstrate Emotional Intelligence.

9. Listen more, talk less.

IV. Live and work in a beautiful environment

The day I placed the *Raiders* of the Lost Ark poster in our bookkeeping office at the home improvement center, Hechingers, the energy changed and every coworker who visited our closet of an office noticed it. During the Covid-19 quarantine, I worked from my living room. Working in front of my mid-century modern floral painting made me so happy that I bought new artwork for my office when we went back to work in-person.

Releasing the Old through Decluttering

The Co-Creation process operates like a vacuum. When we create the space for a new idea, the demonstration of this idea shows up. For this reason, it is very important to create new space both in our minds and in our physical world. Feng Shui is the practice of moving energy throughout our homes and offices, letting go of what no longer serves us so the new shows up and has a place to live. Your first exercise will be to examine the contents of your home and/or office. Answer the following questions:

1. Are you holding on to and using furniture you do not like?
2. Does your home and office nourish your spirit?
3. Is your space welcoming to family, friends, and your desires?
4. Are you keeping photos of former friends or partners that block new opportunities?
5. Does the energy in your home circulate, or is it stagnant or clogged?

Take Action:

- Make a commitment to throw out ten items no longer useful in your life.
- Make a commitment to organize your environment at home and at work.
- Make a commitment to let go of outdated clothing you don't wear or no longer fits you.
- Make your bed every day.
- Cook nourishing foods for yourself.
- Have cut veggies in the fridge for handy salad making
- Stay ahead of your laundry.

- Hire cleaning staff.
- Hire help for the lawn, gardens, or chores too much for you to take care of.
- Make sure your furniture is clean and attractive.
- Add art. You can buy inexpensive posters at the art museum.
- Have your closet redone by an organizer. It makes putting an outfit together easier!
- Put attractive outfits together in advance, or buy your clothes from a boutique or hire a service that can do it for you.
- Learn how to style your hair and makeup. Have a good skincare regimen.
- In the words of Mary Schmich made famous by film director Baz Lurhman, *Wear Sunscreen!* (I have been wearing tinted moisturizer with SPF since my early 20s thanks to my mom's good friend from New Orleans, Louise Murnane).

Entertain Synonyms
Amuse
Regard
Consider
Contemplate
Think About
Give Thought to
Bear in Mind
Think
Believe
Dream
Mull Over
Deliberate
Ponder
Respect

Entertain Antonym
Disregard
Ignore
Take no notice of
Discount
Pay no attention to
Disrespect
Indifference

STEP SIX: ENTERTAIN

"You can't isolate the single agent of change; you can only try to create a favorable environment to coax it into reappearing." ~Lynne McTaggart[24]

Think about all of the possibilities for your future. Pick a few. Invite these ideas in for dinner or a snack. Sit around the table with different possibilities and see how it feels. Think Big about changes that can occur in your life. The Happiness Research from Harvard University[25] shows that if you focus on positive possibilities, it changes your brain for the better. Instead of focusing on the problems, focus on the better life you are seeking. Lynne McTaggart's Intention Experiment created healing environments through remote healing for many, many participants.

There are three different definitions of the word *entertain*:

1. To be hospitable or to host
2. To provide amusement
3. To keep in focus a new possibility

The **Entertain** Step of the model helps you to ponder a new future. This is where we map out our goals and then define the steps necessary to get there. Before we can move forward, we need to contemplate what we are asking to come into our lives. A new job. A new career. A new hobby. A new home. A new relationship. A new city. A new car. The list is endless, but also make sure to include the nonphysical elements of your life.

---

24 Lynne McTaggart, *The Power of Eight*, (New York, NY, Simon & Schuster, 2017), ISBN:978150115547; 9781501115554

- Quality of life
- Peace of mind
- Time to rest
- Happiness
- Doing what you love
- Fulfillment
- Saving the planet
- Giving to others
- Having fun
- Being in partnership
- Living in abundance

The concept of *entertaining* is taking an idea and inviting it into your life. Imagine what it would feel like to achieve your goals. Use your five senses. Imagine what the desired goals look like, sound like, taste like, feel like, and smell like, and act as if it is already so!

Do your research, but most importantly, make some decisions. Don't worry, you can always change your mind later. Do you know anyone who cannot make up their mind about what it is they desire in their future? How successful is that person in life? Desires plus decision equals demonstration.

Watch out for what is known as the "fallacy of sunk costs" which is an economic principle stating that if you have invested heavily into something, you should continue with it, so you don't lose the money. The **Entertain** step of the model coaches us in the opposite direction by supporting us to stop investing in a failed pursuit and preclude any future losses now. I cancelled two trips this year and lost travel deposits. During the time I was supposed to be in Mexico, I became extremely sick and was glad I cancelled the trip. The second trip, a cruise, didn't feel right and interfered with my meeting with the editor for this book. As I recently heard someone say, "If it is right, make it easy; if it is wrong, make it obvious." Follow your gut. As of this writing, I went to Florida instead of the cruise and met with my editor in person. It was the right decision; I lost the deposit of $500 for the cruise, but I did not have to pay the $3,000 I still owed.

If you don't **Clarify** exactly what it is you are seeking and know your priorities, it may not come to fruition. The simple act of deciding on your future makes all the difference in the world. As Ernest Holmes taught, you are attracting into your life exactly what you are thinking about.

Sometimes unexpected things happen in life, and upon reflection, while we may have been wanting a change, we did not take action. In my life, this applies to a few friendships that have gone awry, some lost clients, and the dissolution of my marriage. In each case, I wanted a change, but I just didn't know how to go about it. If I don't make the decision, then someone or something makes it for me. The Universe stepped in and took care of it. And in each of these situations, my quality of life improved because of the change. Once I adapted to the shock of losing the relationship and letting it go, it all happened for good. Dr. Carlton Whitehead, formerly of a Science of Mind Center in Chicago, gave a talk at Asilomar one year on the Aramaic word "Gomzo." Loosely translated, it means "everything happens for good." We may not think so at the moment, but life in retrospect always shows us the good that comes out of situations of loss.

I have struggled in a few jobs that were not a good match. Staying too long only lengthens your problems. Of course, you need to take responsible action and not put yourself at financial risk, but don't stay in a situation or relationship that is just not supporting you.

Your mind is the most powerful tool you have, and you have the ability to direct your thoughts to create the outcomes you desire!

Entertain Story: Pivoting My Business in COVID-19

When COVID-19 became the new reality in March 2020, life changed for us all. The first week of the stay-at-home order in Pennsylvania, I found out that I was under the threat of losing my largest risk management consulting client. We worked harmoniously for 25 years, and it was my main source of income. I felt extremely upset, which I knew was not a good approach. Stress of the kind I experienced can unduly and significantly affect our immune system.

I had a good talking-to with myself and decided to practice the **Clarity Concepts**™ model. I asked myself which step to follow, and I picked Love, which says we should love everything occurring in our life, trust there is a spiritual reason for this occurrence, and find the faith to truly believe something better is on the horizon.

Part of my practice in loving everything is to ask myself, *What is something I am grateful for that can help me right now?* In my head, I mused, *I am grateful that New York Life Insurance Company offered me a job with a base salary and benefits some time ago. I can always restart there.*

I got out my pendulum crystal and checked all seven Chakra energy centers in my body. I added special techniques to clear myself of negative energy, and most importantly, I followed the Five Steps of Affirmative Prayer I shared earlier. Once I surrendered the problem to a greater idea, I proceeded to have an amazing and productive day. I felt inspired.

I went up to my office, and as I walked through the door, my office phone rang. It was startling. Miraculously, a female voice on the phone said, "Hello, this is Sunny Thomas from New York Life. I am calling to check in on members of our women's group."

This was stunning! First of all, I never met or heard of Sunny; she worked for a different office of New York Life than the one I interviewed with. Secondly, I replied I did not need her assistance as I held a Life Insurance Brokerage License. To which she responded, *That's great! We are hiring!*

Later that same day, an email arrived announcing an opening in Risk Management Faculty at Temple University, my alma mater. What jumped out at me was the job required skills I already possessed - not only teaching, but managing the student business fraternity, internships, and career placements. I have managed and participated in many mentoring programs because that is how I practice paying it forward (**Let Go**); however, now, the thought of getting paid for this work was extremely exciting!

I interviewed for both jobs, and after making it to the final four, ultimately the Temple position was put on hold. In the meantime, I turned down the current offer from New York Life and was also offered a job with insurer Chubb, which required me to shut down my business. As it turns out, I was only given a six-month extension on my largest client contract. At first, it was shocking! It forced me to go deep and unearth the cause for the major fear that I was experiencing. While I grew up in an affluent neighborhood, my parents experienced significant financial troubles. That is all I knew. I went from Lord & Taylor clothing to thrift store shopping. It all happened overnight when my father stopped pursuing his career. It was also the 70s, and while the job market was difficult for him, he was possessed by other issues that contributed to his financial challenges.

Here I am, many years later, still working to retrain my mind that *my* financial situation is incredibly different from my dad's. My spiritual philosophies have supported me for years. I am an entrepreneur and am pursuing other opportunities to replace this significant loss of income. I acknowledged that managing this client had become extremely stressful. Much like my marriage and some friendships that have ended, I did not want the client relationship to end, but I desperately wanted the stress to stop and for things to change. Well, it did when SCHOTT's sister company non-renewed my contract. Again, be careful what you are asking for whether knowing or unknowing. It turned out to be the best financial move I could have made because I now spend a lot of time in litigation, which is more financially rewarding.

I put the CC model into action:

Clarity: What is it that I want?

1. Grow my insurance expert witness work to replace the income loss.
2. Find a job in a university environment that allows me to keep my expert witness practice and my independence.
3. Obtain great benefits, including health insurance, with this job.
4. Develop talents as a paid mentor to students and others.
5. Obtain tuition benefits for my son Mackie.
6. Be licensed to sell Property and Casualty Insurance as well as Life Insurance.

Co-Create: Know I have the power to create my desires.

Because my childhood belief system embraced the idea of constant financial stress, I worked with energy healer Lorraine DiGiovanni to release the old Belief System (known as BS by minister Dr. James Mellon). A CSL Practitioner used Affirmative Prayer to know that I am moving far, far away from this old and untrue Belief System. She reminded me that my faith was stronger than the Belief System around money struggles. I just simply needed to remember my connection to Universal Power, and that I live in an abundant and prosperous Universe.

Love: On a daily basis, I practice gratitude in the following ways:

1. For my safety
2. For my son
3. For my son's incredible grade school, St. Katherine of Siena, and now Radnor High School
4. For my family
5. For my friends

6. For my beautiful house
7. For my pool
8. For my tennis club
9. For my kitty Jetson - a healer in his own right
10. For our therapists and healers

Letting Go: As discussed above, I dove into the deep work of letting go of my old belief system around money. I am also letting go of my former partnership and my largest client. I am working hard not to protest these changes but to embrace them.

Embody: When I learned I may lose my biggest client, I applied for three jobs. One is on hold, one I turned down, and one will eventually come to fruition. The other thing I did to **embody** moving forward is to invest in a Google ad for my Expert Witness work and to sign up for intensive training to become an insurance arbitrator. I am also exploring other university positions.

Entertain: I know that other work is coming to me. Just like the undefined new job I asked for before I started my own business, I envision my consulting practice growing by leaps and bounds. To do this, I invested in a Google ad, trained as an Arbitrator, and hired a marketing coach. These were all significant investments to move my business forward.

Love: Gratitude is the key to the **Love** Step of the model. I am also searching for ways to appreciate this challenging time of change. For example, while I am in the middle of divorcing, my son's father has chosen to move to Radnor so my son can be in the High School I wanted for him. I asked my son a few years ago if I should sell my house and move to Radnor, PA, and he said, *No!* Be careful what you wish for! Finding love during these challenging times will pave the way for the stress to subside. It also helps your immune system. Rev. Dr. Jay Scott Neale advises "Love yourself first. Give first to you and then give it away."

Let Go: In times of uncertainty, we all have so much to **let go**. In general, **let go** of old belief systems from the past. **Let go** of or reform relationships that are no longer working for you. **Let go** of frustrations, disappointments, and perceived failures. As Jackson Browne sang, "Let the disappointments pass, let the illusions last until they shatter." Examine your illusions.

Affirm: I have started a few new daily affirmations:

I have a great deal of business and handle it with clarity, focus, ease, and grace.
I am hired by Temple University in the perfect job.
My relationship with my son improves every day.

Attend: Every day, I take a step to move my business forward. I have been advertising, training, and networking. I also pay attention to what I am thinking. Even though we think upwards of 60,000 thoughts a day, most of them are flighty at best. I focus on the positive. I am working with therapists and practitioners to help me reverse any negative thinking that might be holding me back.

Resonate: Pay particular **attention** to the frequency with which you are resonating. Is it happy, calm, and aware? Or is it dark and dirty as exemplified by Masaru Emoto in his book, *Hidden Messages in Water*? I am working on my mindfulness techniques. When I begin to feel scared or agitated, I stop and take deep breaths. I allow myself to cry sometimes. Its best to resonate with faith than with fear. Make room for the positive through prayer, meditation, yoga, exercise, music, dancing, singing, and whatever fills your cup.

Replenish: My weekly commitment to Pilates and meditation is an important part of maintaining my physical and spiritual health and vitality. I also walk, and when it is available to me, I swim and participate in Aqua Fit classes. Right now, as we pivot to safer in-person activities, I am taking Paddle Tennis lessons with my son because we can play outside all year long.

In the end, I successfully kept my largest client. I also became certified as an Insurance Arbitrator, which has significantly increased my network and my income. I invested in advertisements to expand my Expert Witness practice which has blossomed significantly.

The model worked for me. I know it works for you!

Entertain Story: My First Convertible

My husband always reflected fondly about the white Pontiac Le Mans Convertible he owned in graduate school in LA. I have great memories of my Uncle Pete's maroon 1966 Mustang Convertible we drove in summers in Huntington, Long Island. I said, "Let's get a convertible." My husband felt that it would be too expensive, but I asked him to look. He called me one day and said, "You are not going to believe this. I found what we are looking for. It's a 1966 Pontiac Tempest Custom Convertible that has been garaged its whole life in Connecticut." He found it in a one-line written ad in *Hemings Motor News*. We bought the car, named it Frankie, and knew immediately it was EXACTLY what we were looking for. We enjoyed many years of good fun with her. Why did we get a deal on the car? The owner wanted it to go to a family who would not convert her into a GTO. This car was such a deal that my friend, who was looking for a 1966, offered me $2,000 more than I paid a week after Frankie came home. I loved that car until the brakes malfunctioned, and we sold the car to a mechanic who could fix the problem. Below is a photo of me in the car with my son.

Entertain Story: My Second Convertible

I attended a business dinner with a colleague who had driven up in her Volvo hardtop convertible. I have owned a few beloved Volvos in my time and have been to their factory in Gothenburg, Sweden. I wanted that car. "Yes," my colleague said, "but Volvo doesn't make this model anymore." When I returned home, I started searching and found the exact same car she was driving with only 50,000 miles on it. It was at a dealership owned by the company my brother served for 30 years. He told me to wait until the General Manager came in, and before we could negotiate, the car was sold.

Instead of being upset, I **let go**. "Okay," I told my brother, "I am going to look at a BMW because your group also has a BMW dealership" Every month, I would look for an older BMW convertible with a hard top. Finally, I found one! It was a 2011 BMW 328i with a hardtop with only 65,000 miles on it. If you know anything about BMWs, they will last forever if you take care of them. Some people have told me this is the best engine BMW ever made. My other brother was driving a 2010 328i sedan and loved it. Because I was family, the General Manager at the dealership was very generous, and I was able to purchase this magnificent car for a great price. I simply love it, and more importantly, I feel happy when I drive it. Here is a photo of my BMW with my son, now much older than he was in the picture in Frankie.

Entertain Story: My Two-Year Life Plan

Paine Webber in their Manhattan-based Risk Management Department hired me right out of college, earning a highly competitive salary. I was fortunate to get this job. As I mentioned, I told everyone there were no Risk Management jobs in Philadelphia, and I would probably have to go New York City. Was I right or did I create this outcome? At the time, there were no Risk Management Philadelphia-based jobs open at my level.

Our department was unique because of our dual role. Our primary job was the procurement of insurance for PaineWebber; secondarily, we reported into PW's subsidiary insurance brokerage unit. We attended regular training meetings and enjoyed yearly Christmas parties with the insurance brokerage unit located out-side of Baltimore.

During one of our off-site meetings, we were given an index card and instructed to write down our two-year career goals and put them in an envelope. For three years, I lived in the New York Metro area and was ready to return to Philadelphia. I felt guilty as I wrote:

1. Relocate to Philadelphia
2. Transfer to the Paine Webber Risk Management unit in Philadelphia
3. Make over $50,000 a year

We gave the envelope to the Senior Vice President of the group, and she prom-ised to return them to us, unopened, in two years. The important challenge to this plan is that at the time of my writing, Paine Webber Risk Management only had two offices: one in Baltimore and my office in NYC was the other.

Not long after this meeting, Paine Webber sold our group to a larger insurance brokerage, The Hobbs Group. A year after the sale, I moved into a sales role at Hobbs. This was an exciting time! When I moved into my role as an Insurance Brokerage Account Executive, I worked on large accounts such as Ryobi Tools, Days Inn, and the New York Stock Exchange.

Being in sales was fun because of the perquisites (perks). Our training meetings were held offsite at luxurious resorts. This elegance became part of the fabric of my life. We experienced Cape Cod and the Biltmore in Phoenix, Arizona. These events were incredibly luxurious and remain treasured memories from this time as was a personal performance by Ray Charles in a small room at the Biltmore.

After almost two years in sales with Hobbs Group, the regional Vice President asked me if I would like to transfer to the Philadelphia office of Hobbs Group. Not only was I asked to move home, but I was also able to negotiate a relocation package that covered the $5,000 cost to pack and transport my belongings to Pennsylvania.

Imagine my surprise when I was delivered an envelope at the next-offsite meeting simply labeled "Jane Downey" in my own handwriting. I opened it up and there it was:

Relocate to Philadelphia with Hobbs Group at a certain salary.

I realized all three of my goals. And honestly, I did not remember setting the intention in writing. I just knew what I wanted to **Co-Create**. As my nephew recently said, "The Universe is really conspiring to support us." This insight comes naturally; he has never studied the Science of Mind.

Entertain: The Making of the Canvas Labyrinths for the Year 2000

In 1999, I travelled to Racine, Wisconsin, for a retreat with Veriditas, the group formerly part of Grace Cathedral that certified me as a Labyrinth Facilitator. During the weekend retreat, there was a global call for the world to walk the labyrinth on New Year's Eve as we welcomed in the new century. I decided to make a canvas with the 36-foot Chartres Cathedral labyrinth pattern. Unbeknownst to me, this style of labyrinth pattern is hard work and time intensive, and a canvas of that size retails for over $4,000.

At the event, my friends introduced a new and revised pattern styled after the Chartres Cathedral pattern. Because it is very difficult to find an area that has 36 feet of uninterrupted space without columns, doors, or walls, the labyrinth was reduced in size to 24 feet. While the smaller canvas was preferable, I already purchased the blank canvas in the larger size. Unbelievably, my 60-year-old friend helped cut and sew the 36-foot canvas. It is made in two pieces with Velcro down the center. She used an industrial sewing machine, and we were able to craft the canvas in her home.

Once we crafted the 36-foot canvas for the Chartres Labyrinth replica, we discovered that there was just enough canvas left over to make the 24-foot canvas that I knew would be much easier to use due to its smaller size. It was a miracle akin to the Bible story of the loaves and the fishes that multiplied to feed everyone. We made the second canvas and then shipped them off to my friends who created the sacred geometrical pattern of the labyrinth to an exact match of Chartres on the 36-foot canvas and the Chartres derivative on the 24-foot canvas. I gathered a group of helpful friends, and we painted the two canvases in my basement and in the basement of another friend.

My next task was to find a place to host the Walk for Peace. I contacted the head of Upper Merion Parks and Recreation, and he welcomed the idea. We hosted the event at the old Gulph Mills school building, and for ten consecutive years, we held the event on New Year's Eve. It was a magical time (See photo of Mel and Sam on labyrinth with me).

Once I set the intention to create a labyrinth and host the New Year's Eve walk, the idea was set in motion through Universal Energy to make it all happen quite easily. I still have the 24-foot canvas, which we are starting to use again as the pandemic wanes.

Entertain Story: The Ruby Ring

My maternal grandfather wore a gold and ruby pinky ring. At some point, my mother inherited it and gave it to me. I put it in what I thought was a *safe* place. Months later, I received a call from my brother who just returned from a dangerous tour of duty with the US Army in Iraq. He inquired about the ring and told me our mother had actually given it to him. I did not tell him I had no clue as to the whereabouts of the ruby ring.

I went into a panic and began a search of the house. It was not in my jewelry box or anyplace I would have logically put a gold and ruby ring. So, I resorted to Spirit. Going back to my Catholic roots, I completed a prayer to Saint Anthony:

St. Anthony, St. Anthony, please come around. Something is lost and must be found.

Then, I sat quietly and went into a meditative state, completing an Affirmative Prayer Treatment, in which I declared the ring is already found. I'm not sure why I was so upset about not finding the ring earlier. Clearly, I did not want to disappoint my brother.

Hours later, the ruby ring appeared in the middle of my living room floor. How it got there, I do not know! I had not seen it in months, but because I **entertained** the idea that the ring would appear, this is exactly what happened. There is a saying, "There is nothing ever lost in the Mind of God." I believed this to be true, and it was. Miracles can happen!

Years later, I went to see Theresa Caputo, the Long Island Medium, in Atlantic City. Theresa brings messages from those who have passed away. She spoke about how spirits who have passed may move small items, like jewelry, around in your home. It made me think of my grandfather, and I wondered if his spirit moved the ring for me to find. Not minutes later, Theresa asked the audience, "Who has the ruby pinky ring?" Although the reading was not for me, I was convinced it was a message from my grandfather letting me know he was there.

My grandfather was extremely strong. He was a pioneer and moved his wife and daughter from Green Bay, Wisconsin, to Los Angeles, CA, to help strengthen my grandmother's health in a more temperate climate. He was 25 percent Native American and a large, strapping man. When he was unable to find work during the Great Depression, he travelled to Saudi Arabia and earned income laying pipeline for the oil companies. He was a survivor. His message was always *It will all work out!*

Entertain Story: A New *Partner*

In January of 2002, I flew to San Francisco to participate in the Veriditas Labyrinth Facilitator Reunion at Grace Cathedral. I knew inherently I needed to go, even though there was no clear reason for this choice. The program was rescheduled because of the events of September 11, 2001. I lived in New York at that time and knew a number of people who died on 9/11. My brother's desk at the Pentagon did not survive, but fortunately, he did as he was out of town. In the months following this tragic day, I spent time studying my life and what was important for me going forward. My desire for a romantic partnership was part of my focus. This analysis started during a solo trip to Germany; but somehow, I knew I could continue the deep internal work I needed to complete while walking the labyrinth in the quiet and support of Grace Cathedral.

I phoned my friend in San Francisco's Noe Valley who offered me his guest bedroom. When I called to check scheduling, he told me he had a new roommate.

He wanted me to extend my stay and come see them both. I booked myself at the Hilton for two nights and then arranged to stay with Dave and his new flat mate after that. After San Francisco, I planned to jet to Houston to visit my annual Labyrinth Society Gathering roommate. I phoned my brother, a United Airlines' pilot, and arranged for standby flights. This was the first time I ever used his employee privileges, and the flexibility of these tickets proved to be crucial to my journey. In hindsight, these arrangements simply clicked into place.

All went well on my flight out. I watched a lovely John Cusack movie entitled *Serendipity* on the plane about the love destined between a man from New York and a woman who ultimately ended up in San Francisco. It foreshadowed my upcoming labyrinth experience.

I was thrilled to discover that two of my favorite labyrinth friends, the ones who had drawn my canvas labyrinths, chose to attend as well. *What a treat*, I thought, *now I know why I made the trip.* The Friday evening at Grace Cathedral was enchanting. The church was transformed by candlelight, and we entered to walk the labyrinth and come together in a ritual. Rev. Lauren instructed us to circle around the labyrinth, and one by one step onto the canvas and cite our intent. *Partner,* I declared, and Destiny, the Harpist, echoed it throughout the Cathedral.

Partner, Partner, Partner, Partner

This process engaged all steps of the **Clarity Concepts**™ model: Clarity, Co-Creation, Love and Letting Go, Attention, Affirmation, Embodiment, the Entertainment of a new future, and Resonance and Replenishment on the labyrinth. One hour later, I found myself outside of Grace Cathedral in a dreamlike state. I didn't want to lose the sacredness of the ritual, so I called my friend Dave, telling him I would not be attending his party that night. In stern and cajoling tones, he said I had to attend. I hailed a cab and wondered the entire trip why I was bothering since I planned to see Dave in two days.

That night, at the party, I met Ron, my first husband. Within an hour or so of my powerful declaration, with the support of the labyrinth, our group, and our harpist, the two of us were introduced. I am not sure what magic was sprinkled on this wonderful day or the effect of "receiving warmth" on our transformative labyrinth, but we were together for 17 mostly happy years.

Ron and I met for an amazing lunch the next day; the air was full of signs and signals of our togetherness. I glimpsed a sign under the freeway that said:

I knew Something Wonderful was about to happen.

The next morning, I packed to leave and Ron said sweetly, "You know, you could stay a few days."

My tickets were standby, but I told him I planned to meet my friend Mary Beth in Houston. "Well," he said, "maybe something will happen at the airport."

My host Dave worked at SFO airport, so he rode with me to my flight. As we pulled into the United terminal, there were thousands of people milling in front of the terminal. We soon discovered the entire United terminal was closed because of a security issue. I called United and was told, "Honey, you can leave tomorrow." I called Mary Beth, who said she had seen it on national news, and then I announced to Ron that I was staying another day. When I told him the story of the airport closure, he joked, "That would be my people at work on your behalf!"

On the way back to his apartment, I saw an advertisement that read: *Keep her away from your roommate!*

Ron and I made a special trip to Grace Cathedral to walk the labyrinth, and in the car, we heard Tony Bennett on the radio singing about leaving his heart in San Francisco. At this point, it seemed as if the angels interceded. The extra day in San Francisco was crucial in our developing bond. I finally left for Houston on Thursday, and by the time I returned to Philadelphia, I was madly in love. Our long-distance relationship flourished, and Ron moved East seven months later. We married and share one magnificent son. On Christmas that year, we went to Grand Rapids, Michigan, for the holidays. Ron's parents' church, St. Mark's Episcopal, was hosting a labyrinth walk in the evening. I attended with Ron's sister and brother-in-law and found, much to my delight, it was the inaugural walk on a canvas made by my friends Stu and Mary! The synchronicity was stunning as the circle continued! It affirmed for me that I was in the right place and was at home even though, for the first time in my life, I was away from my family for Christmas. As I look back, the twists and turns of our romance and partnership followed the paths of the labyrinth. We looked forward, following the way; although at times, it was difficult to see what life would bring around the bend to help blend our bicoastal lives. The labyrinth not only brought this circumstance, these friends, this experience; it showed us the way!

Entertain Exercises:

I. Put your desires into action and try something on for size!

1. If you wish to buy a house at the beach, go and rent one so you can explore the area.
2. If you think you know what career interests you, go meet with people in that industry and do informational interviews. This process can be incredibly helpful in guiding you to the right choice. As I have told my son, meeting with the college fencing teams and coaches will help to guide him to the right university.
3. Expand your options when you are considering something new.
4. Journal how you feel about different opportunities. More than twice, I have turned down job opportunities that just did not feel right or conflicted with another plan.

II. Draw a map of your future

Drawing, painting, and creating art is a wonderful way to get in touch with what your true desires really are. Use art to create a visual of what your career and life path will look like. Right now, mine would include a new partner with fabulous grandchildren frolicking in my pool

III. Examine your patterns/uproot negative Core Beliefs

1. Make a list of the patterns and situations in your life which are not supporting your goals.
2. Develop an Action Plan as to how you are going to release these circumstances from your life.
3. Write out what you want your life to look like (Entertain).
4. Make a list of the excuses you often use to avoid dealing with these changes.
5. Is there anything you need to complete or take action on to move forward in this change?

Affirm Synonyms
Assert
Insist
Confirm
Avow
Announce
Pronounce
Acknowledge

Affirm Antonyms
Refute
Disprove
Contest
Rebut
Prove False

STEP SEVEN: AFFIRM

The Prayer of Jabez: A Daily Prayer
Oh, that you would bless me indeed
And expand my territory
May your hand be with me
And may I do no harm.[26]

This step of the **Clarity Concepts**™ model provides you with useful tools. Now that you have spent some time clearing your mind of negative messages, you can replace or overwrite any remaining self-doubts or blockages with a mantra of what it is you are seeking. I often use affirmations as prayers.

Some examples of Affirmations include:

- A new job is coming to me.
- The Universe supports me.
- I only experience loving relationships.

An oft-quoted metaphysical saying by Napoleon Hill goes like this: "Whatever the mind can conceive and believe, it can achieve."

The purpose of affirmations is to rewrite any negative messaging embedded in your subconscious mind. Think of it like rewriting computer coding.

For example, I grew up with my parents constantly worrying that they did not have enough money. Even though I am highly successful, I often find myself

---

26 1 Chronicles 4:10, KJV

worrying about money and my future income. To reframe this negative thinking, I created an affirmation:

I live in an abundant and prosperous universe.

Our goals do change and should be malleable just as our world is constantly changing. The most important part of Holme's teaching is "the law of giving and receiving" or the "law of circulation." This concept asks us to give back to what spiritually supports us. This could be a charity, a church, a supportive friend or family member, a yoga center or anything you think gives back to society. The Bible teaches that as you give, it will be returned to you multiplied abundantly, pressed down, and overflowing.

How to Write an Affirmation using Positive Words to Convince Your Subconscious Mind

Begin with acknowledging that you are open to a positive future. Begin your affirmations with trusting words such as:

I know; I believe; I trust; I have faith; I have conviction.

As Shakti Gawain taught in *Creative Visualization*, remember to add to the end of your affirmation:

This or something better manifests.

This allows room for a greater outcome. The subconscious mind does not understand time and space. When you relive a past hurt over and over, it becomes an active resentment, and you are reliving the hurt every day and keeping it alive. That is why forgiveness is so powerful. If you can release some hurt and worry from the past, you leave room to focus on the present, planning for the future, and moving gracefully forward. Using a Vision Board or a Treasure Map of photographs of what you desire, such as money, a relationship, health, vitality, and employment, are ways to cement these desires in the subconscious mind.

Affirmations must always be written in the present tense, be positive, personal, and precise. Tips on how you should write your affirmation include using:

- Using I AM or I HAVE which is a sacred blessing to Spirit
- Words specific to you
- Short and to the point
- Open-ended
- Knowing truth
- Living into your goal/belief
- Bumping your belief *"up a notch"*
- Believable
- Convincing

The following is not an affirmation because it contains negative concepts. Afirmations are present tense, positive, personal, and precise statements. Ernest Holmes said, *"Hope is the subtle illusion and unconscious compromise."* Hope presumes the possibility of not realizing what you have affirmed.

I hope I will get a job to pay the bills.

Use Positive Words:

Deserving	Creative	Strong	Accepting	Willing
Affirming	Knowing	Plugged-in	Juice	

Use just one or two affirmations for the week. I am currently working with:

I am living my perfect life.
My willpower is strong as I create healthy new habits.
I forgive myself for past mistakes.
I release my anger toward myself and others.

Affirmation Story: Swim and Tennis Club

Martins Dam private swim and tennis club required four referral letters to join. Our township pool was in disarray, and it appeared unclean. After taking my young son for a play date at the township pool, I was disturbed by the condition of the swim club. I declared to my husband, "I am getting the last referral letter to Martins Dam club today!" Now, I was focused. Later that afternoon,

I facilitated a labyrinth walk at St. Peter's Church in Great Valley. One of the participants I had never met referenced her swim club. I quickly asked her if she belonged to the Martins Dam Club in Wayne, and she confirmed she did. My final letter was arranged that day. My new friend even hand-delivered the entire application to the Membership Chair. We are still friends to this day, and the club has been meaningful to my family through tennis, paddle tennis, and swim team. And now, my 15-year-old son works there. He earned enough to pay for his hotel room in Salt Lake City because he wanted to stay an extra day for a fencing match!

Affirmation Story: New Job for the Plumber

Our toilet pump needed repairing, and I hired a plumber. I must admit I was shocked to find out in conversation that he was into metaphysics. I learned this when I asked if he was happy with his employer, Newco. He said, "Absolutely yes." He went on to say, "While in my last job, I told my wife I needed to find a new firm. That very same day, I received a call from Newco saying they were very impressed with my resume and wanted to interview me for a position. I asked the recruiter for the date of the resume. I posted it on Monster over 10 years ago!" He received the call the day he made the declaration. Our demonstrations do not often manifest with such speed; however, when the employee and the employer are aligned and on the same wave length, anything is possible!

Affirmation Story: My Travel to Hawaii and Guam

Years ago, my mother relocated to Guam. She was pestering me to come for a visit. I am not a big fan of long plane flights. My mom and I experienced a contentious relationship and have known conflict, so I was hesitant to make the journey. None of my siblings wanted to go.

I declared, "I am going to Guam with two conditions: I have a travelling companion, and I get to stay a week in Hawaii."

A few weeks later at a dinner party, my friend asked, "Does anyone want to go to Maui? I have enough Marriott points for a week in Kaanapali Beach." I said, "Yes, if you will go to Guam with me!"

Not only did I manifest the traveling companion and the free stays in Hawaii and Guam, but I also had enough Delta Airline points for a free trip!

Affirm Exercises:

I. **Write your Affirmations. Go back to one of your first exercises and look at the negative messaging you wrote down. Now, design some affirmations to turn that "stinking" thinking around:**

    I am worthy...

    I now know and believe ...

    I am attracting ...

    I am magnetizing ...

    My vision for the future includes ...

    The purpose of affirmation is to address negative core beliefs such as:

    I am not worthy into an affirmation of: *I am worthy of fine things*

    I could have done more into an affirmation of: *I always do my best, and I am a hard worker.*

II. **Write an inventory of the things you love to do.**

    *   Work flexibility
    *   Variety at work
    *   Leading a team
    *   Providing insight
    *   Writing
    *   Looking at art
    *   Visiting a great museum
    *   Fine dining
    *   Good wine

- Being with friends
- Attending a concert or sporting event
- Reading a great book

III. List favorite things, desires, and your bucket list. Design some affirmations around those goals. The following are some good affirmations you can turn into your own:

I trust in my future and know a _____ is coming to me.

I know spirit is supporting me as I _____.

I am lovable; I am loved; I am love.

I gently release the past and move forward into my future.

I am spirit in action and know _____."

I am deserving of a loving relationship, because I am lovable. these in quotes?

I am now open to Good and receiving my _____.

I am in the right place at the right time.

I am strong and brave as I _____."

The Universe conspires to support me and my future.

Attend Synonyms
Be Present At
Go To
Listen
Concentrate
Focus
Keep your Mind on
Take
Grasp
Obtain

Attend Antonyms
Forget
Miss
Overlook
Let Pass
Tolerate
Fail to See
Neglect
Ignore
Lose
Pine for

STEP EIGHT: ATTEND

"We may not be able to directly create something we want, but we can still encourage the underlying processes that will bring it into being. Knowing this brings a sense of both responsibility and peace. In terms of responsibility, it's on each of us to tend to the causes that we can influence. Take some time to consider major areas of your life such as health and relationships and look for simple realistic things you could to that would cause them to improve."

—Rick Hanson[27]

The Eighth Step in the Clarity model is to **attend** or to pay attention. Pay attention to:

1. Your Physical Reality

- Your desires
- Your thoughts
- Your activities
- Your friends
- Your family
- Your work environment
- Your diet
- Your home
- Your relationships

27 Rick Hanson, PhD, *Resilient: How to Grow an Unshakable Core of Calm, Strength, and Happiness* (New York: Penguin Random House, 2018). ISBN 978-0-451-49885-4

2. Your Emotions

- Your anger
- Your fears
- Your worry
- Your Joy
- Your sense of self-satisfaction
- Your self-criticism

When you approach your life with laser focus, you soon learn to discern what is supporting you and what is draining your energy and attention. If you are not focused on the positive, you fail to notice opportunities, neglect your growth, and ignore opportunities for expanded change and financial abundance. When I am in a stressful situation in my life, I don't deal with my money stuff as well as I do at other times and losses occur unconsciously.

Keep a watchful eye out for distractions and addictive behavior. Most addictions are a coping mechanism for past traumas and avoiding painful feelings. Find a way to process and move through these patterns of behavior that take you away from your Best Self. I tend to drink too much wine at night to assuage the stress; however, I am much better coping with the stress when I take a walk in the woods or do Pilates or Yoga.

The secret of harmony and success is to concentrate your thoughts upon harmony and success. This why I teach that **attention** is the key to life. What you **attend** to or concentrate upon, you bring into your life because you are building a Mental Equivalent of the desired outcome.

This process includes not criticizing others or situations. It means you must avoid sarcasm and other feigned ways of sharing a complaint. Shockingly, in an article by Travis Bradberry, he states that research shows most people complain once a minute during a typical conversation. Really? He believes complaining is not good for you, so there is scientific evidence behind Dr. James Mellon's *No Complaining Practice* which you will soon be assigned.

Bradberry goes on to say that your brain loves efficiency and doesn't like to work any harder than it has to. When you repeat a behavior, such as complaining, your nexus branches out to each other to ease the flow of information. Thus, complaining rewires your brain for negativity. Stanford University concluded that complaining damages other areas of the brain as well. Complaining also causes the hippocampus portion of the brain to shrink! The hippocampus regulates emotion and is associated with long-term memory. Bradberry's position is that complaining is bad for your health. My position is that complaining will literally create negative outcomes in your life.[28]

Bradberry recommends what he calls Solution-Oriented Complaining, which is incredibly like the tenets of the Clarity Concepts™ model:

- Clear Purpose (Clarify)
- Know Your Outcome (Co-Create)
- Start with Something Positive (Love)
- Be Specific (Entertain)
- Close with something positive (Let Go)

Attend Story: Pat the Pilot

My brother Pat has always known he wanted to fly airplanes. I remember him reading the biography of Eddie Rickenbacker, World War I flying Ace, when he was just five years old. Pat engineered his entire life around his goal to fly planes. Although life as a child was not always easy for him, Pat always embraced a sense of strength because he knew where he was headed. Man, was he focused!

Our father was an Air Force Navigator, and we grew up swimming at Willow Grove Naval Air Station. Everyone's father was a pilot or navigator, so it is no coincidence that many of my swim teammates became pilots, including my other brother Christopher.

Pat carefully watched his grades in high school so he could get into the right college. He obtained a Naval ROTC scholarship at the University of Pennsylvania when he attended Drexel University. When his grades plummeted, Pat moved out of his fraternity to avoid distractions to his goal. He made the Dean's list the following semester. Pat knew what he wanted, and he paid attention to where he put his time, energy, and focus.

---

28 Travis Bradberry, "How to Break a Habit for Good," February 3, 2017, Entrepreneur.com, https://www.entrepreneur.com/growing-a-business/how-to-break-a-bad-habit-for-good/281118.

Ultimately, Pat was accepted into Naval Flight School. No small feat since only a small percentage of graduating naval officers are given this opportunity. Pat ultimately became an A-6 pilot, successfully mastering the landings on aircraft carriers. He then went on to teach young pilots at Meridian. He retired from teaching but still flies for a major airline.

Attend Story: Mackie's Conception

My husband and I met when I was in my late 30s. He had two daughters from a previous marriage, and as a result, we encountered stress concerning custody and parenting issues. He really wanted us to have a child together. I hesitated because I knew what a huge commitment and responsibility raising a child could be. I am the oldest of five children and fully understood the work and challenges of parenting.

We consulted a genetic counselor early in our marriage, and I realize now her advice was somewhat cavalier. Basically, she said there was plenty of time for us to conceive, and she reviewed the risk factors for what the medical community deems pregnancy in "Advanced Maternal Age." Thus, we decided to wait and did not begin focusing on having a child until I was 43 years old. A year went by, and we still had not conceived, so we consulted a fertility clinic.

The clinic was a challenging experience. The testing was not scheduled by appointment, so I would have to arrive at 7:00 a.m. so as to avoid conflict with my workday, and I often waited as much as 90 minutes to get tested. The whole environment of the clinic was stressful and really not conducive to supporting a calm approach to pregnancy. I also developed a bad reaction to a commonly prescribed fertility drug and felt it interfered with my chances to get pregnant. At this point, I decided to move to another clinic. My physician from the clinic, Dr. Schnapp, called me, clearly angry that I was leaving. When I told her that the drug caused problems for me, she said, "No, it was not the drug. You are perimenopausal and will need an egg donor!" It was a shocking pronouncement, and I was stunned. I burst into tears and began thinking, *Do I ask my sister for an egg? How does that work? Would she be willing? Would it be awkward to have kids that were half siblings?* I was very upset.

We went to the new clinic my neighbor insisted upon. The energy was incredibly different. The office ran like clockwork, they kept all of their appointments on time, and every member of the staff was compassionate and encouraging. The doctor we met with told us to keep an open mind. He encouraged us to embark on hormone therapy to increase our chances, and we proceeded accordingly.

In the meantime, I was introduced to an energy healer. I set up a phone appointment with Sharon to work on some issues I was having with my stomach. I have studied the healing arts for years and feel it is integral to living a healthy life. Trapped energy, anger, and discord can create disease in the physical body. When Sharon worked on me, I mentioned we were trying to get pregnant. At the end of the call, she said she would check in with the Healing Temple she accesses for particularly challenging issues. A day later, she phoned and told me the Temple wanted to take my fertility case. She explained, "It will cost $3,000! The Temple team will receive your cash and place it on their altar. They will pray on your case 24 hours a day until you manifest the child you so desire." Their cost was much less than the medical fertility intervention, and my husband and I agreed to give it a try. The real reason I worked with the Healing Temple is because the first doctor planted the negative seed thought into my head concerning inability to conceive. I truly believe that our thoughts create our reality, and I needed to find a way to overpower this worry she tried to instill in me.

I met Sharon at the bank and gave her 30 $100 bills. The first step, Sharon told me, was to clear my house of any energy interfering with conception. My healer friends came over, and they decided the bookcase in our bedroom presented some negative energy. It contained my husband's antique book collection, and I set about clearing the energy with sage. Thinking our job was complete, I called Sharon. She asked me to walk to my bedroom while we were on the phone.

"What is to the left as you walk in the room?"

"That's the bookcase I was telling you about."

"What is behind the bookcase?" I told her it was my husband's closet.

We have a dressing room separated from the bedroom which contains the bathroom vanity and two large closets. Now, Sharon had never been to my home. This examination of my home was done remotely and through her psychic insight.

"Well," she proclaimed, "there is something in your husband's closet."

"What could possibly be in his clothing closet?" I challenged.

"I had a client who was having marital issues, and we discovered that her wedding dress from a prior marriage was energetically interfering with her current marriage."

"Oh, that could be the culprit. My husband still has his Armani tuxedo from his first marriage. I refused to let him wear it at our wedding."

I immediately phoned my husband, and when he returned home from work that evening, he hauled out a bag of clothes, shoes, ties, etc. that had been given to him by his ex-wife or his ex-mother-in-law. It was funny as I didn't like any of the articles of clothing he removed and was happy to see them leave. He did keep the tuxedo, but it was relocated down to a coat closet next to the side entrance to our house.

Within two months of clearing the closet, we were pregnant with our own biological child! My son even has my husband's crooked pinky fingers to prove it. I learned later that, statistically, we only had an 8 percent chance of having a child with my egg, including in vitro fertilization. The difference is that we set a clear intention, and with our Higher Power at work on our behalf, success was a given!

Attend Exercise:

I. Using Your Senses

As humans, we receive information through our senses. Unfortunately, during childhood, we are trained to follow "the rules" designed by our primary care givers (parents, teachers, etc.). As adults our innate ability to gather and process information takes over. The following exercises teach you how to laser focus your attention. The more you practice these, the better you become at managing and understanding your thought processes, hearing your still soft voice, and where you are placing your precious attention.

Today's exercise helps you return to your inner-knowing by exercising your senses. It's fun to do this exercise with a friend. You will need the following:

1. Bottle of peppermint oil
2. Cotton Ball
3. Orange Juice
4. Apple Juice

5. Rock song

6. New Age music (Look for Stephen Halpern songs)

7. A soft blanket

II. Exploring Consciousness through the Use of Your Sense of Smell

Take some different essential oils such as peppermint, lavender, and bergamot and close your eyes as you inhale each deeply. What do you smell?

Mint? Earth? Flowers? Love? Freedom? Summer? California? The Beach?

Now rub the oil on your hands and smell again. Did the smell of the oil change properties?

Essential oils are a great way to create a sense of calm and ease. I highly recommend you experiment with them and keep a sniffer in your car or pocketbook. Try and inhale some lavender when someone cuts you off in traffic.

III. Consciousness through the Use of Your Sense of Taste

Taste is affected by smell. First, take a sip of orange juice with your nose plugged up. How did it taste?

Now, take a deep sniff of the juice before you take a taste. What is the difference?

Then, have your friend give you a sip of one of the juices without your knowing which one it is. How is the taste different?

_____

What happens if you take a sip of orange juice, and you think its apple juice? How does your body react? How does the taste change?

_____

IV. Stop Complaining!

This exercise comes from my friend Rev. Dr. James Mellon who insists in his class the first thing his students must do is to spend a week avoiding complaining at all costs. It's really fascinating when you pay **Attention** to every single word you utter. As mentioned previously, this practice is backed by scientific research at Stanford University.

For the next two weeks, take your journal with you and write down the number of times you started to complain. Don't write down the complaint, which would only give it more power; simply write a hash mark to take inventory on the number of times over 14 days you started a complaint. Also, journal how it felt after 14 days of non-complaining.

V. Practice these Relaxation Breath Exercises

Controlling our breathing is one of the easiest and best ways to quiet the mind and reconnect all of your subpersonalities with your core and with Spirit. When you pay attention to your breath, it is all you can focus on. In doing so, you trigger the parasympathetic nervous system which is calming and healing. Here are a number of ways to control your breath. Begin in a comfortable, seated or prone position.

Focus Breath: Breathe in through the nose, breathing in peace, and breathe out through the mouth, releasing stress/angst/worry/concern.

Lion's Breath Yogic breathing: Breathe in through the nose then open your mouth and stick out your tongue exhale quickly, deeply, and loudly through the mouth while saying Ha.

Countdown Breathing: Inhale and count ten, exhale and count nine, inhale and count eight, exhale and count seven, inhale and count six, exhale and count five, inhale and count four, exhale and count three, inhale and count two exhale and count one.

Abdominal Breathing: Notice the way a baby breathes. Instead of a chest breath, the baby breathes in deeply and expands the abdomen. Put one hand on your heart and the other hand on your stomach and slowly inhale through the nose, pushing the air so your stomach rises, then exhale slowly through the mouth or nose.

Alternate Nostril Breathing: This is a Sanskrit breathing technique wherein you use your thumb to close your right nostril and breathe in for four counts, then use your ring finger to close your left nostril, wait a breath with both nostrils closed, and then open the right nostril and breathe out for four counts and repeat. It is recommended to complete at least seven rounds.

Resonate Synonyms
Reverberate
Vibrate
Resound
Ring
Echo
Boom

Resonate Antonyms
Still
Statue-like
Motionless
At rest
Silent
Vacuum

STEP NINE: RESONATE

"God, grant me the serenity
to accept the things I cannot change,
the courage to change the things I can,
and the wisdom to know the difference.
Living one day at a time,
enjoying one moment at a time;
accepting hardship as a pathway to peace;
taking, as Jesus did,
this sinful world as it is,
not as I would have it;
trusting that You will make all things right
if I surrender to Your will;
so that I may be reasonably happy in this life
and supremely happy with You forever in the next.

Amen".

—Reinhold Niebuhr, *The Serenity Prayer* (In its entirety)

At what frequency are you resonating? There seems to be a lot of negativity in this world as I write this. Sadly, there always has been if this is our tendency of thought. To create a happy life, the key is to learn how to handle the stress and not wallow in it. This is why changing your frequency is so important.

There are many exercises in this book that teach you how to uplift one's frequency. According to the psychosynthesis model of psychology, the challenge is to keep all of your subpersonalities connected. Don't go "out on a limb" and get stuck in a trauma memory from years ago. It will change your behavior and create unpleasant outcomes. Increasing your frequency also enables you to take advantage of the **law of attraction.** This means you attract opportunities and relationships with the same frequency in which you are operating. It is the most important reason to replenish. Keep your thoughts and your heart clean and positive.

An article in *Medical News Today*[29] chronicles the links between neuroscience and the immune system. This was merely a theory when I studied Expressive Arts Therapy years ago. Now, psychoneuroimmunology (PNI), the inherent ability of the body to heal itself through positive thinking, is well documented. This field of study was created by Robert Ader and Nicholas Cohen as they studied the effects of stimuli on rats. They found that even when the actual poison was removed, if the stimuli remained, the mortality rate rose significantly. This tells us that the stress in our lives is affecting our bodies.

Another approach to understanding personal relationships is to understand there are many different personalities. I studied this both in corporate negotiations training and in my Spiritual Psychology certification program. Not everyone is gregarious, analytical, shy, or attentive. This is the nature of today's diversity and inclusion programs. Research is showing that healthier, high performing groups have different talents, cultures, and approaches to the world. The more different a group is in meshing their various ideas, the more creative and productive the group will be.

The **Clarity Concepts** Model encompasses Ernest Holme's method of affirmative prayer:

- Begin by knowing that you have the power to **create.**
- **Clarify** your thoughts and intentions.
- **Love** everything in your world.
- **Let Go** of what no longer serves you.

---

29 Tim Newman, "Psychoneuroimmunology: Laugh and Be Well," February 3, 2016, *Medical News Today*, https://www.medicalnewstoday.com/articles/305921.

- **Embody** the outcomes you desire.
- **Entertain** new possibilities for your life.
- **Affirm** the good.
- Pay **attention** to your actions and desires.
- Go into a prayerful state **resonate**, and connect with your higher power.
- This process alone will help you **replenish**.

Note: The science behind how prayer affects the brain is in the **Replenish** section of the book.

When we focus our consciousness directly on people and events we love, we **resonate** at a brighter and happier level. Write down what motivates you. Here is my list:

1. Idea creation
2. Good wine
3. Thank-you notes
4. Motivated people
5. Being with friends
6. Great food
7. Connecting people
8. Any beach
9. Any body of water
10. Swimming
11. Coastal California
12. Walking in the woods
13. Mountains

Resonance also means being in touch with our senses. Take note that the sense of smell is the closest sense to the amygdala part of our brain. This is known as the reptilian brain and is responsible for the fight/flight response. That is why a certain smell can take you back. The smell of bacon always reminds me of my Aunt Lena and her cast iron skillet. It also reminds me of the train station in Hoboken and bacon breakfasts at the shore my brother-in-law carefully cooks for us. Use resonance to change how you may be reacting to a triggered memory through a smell.

One method of healing through resonance is Homeopathy. The father of Homeopathy was Samuel Hahnemann. He was a German physician who hypothesized that your cure to your ailment is your symptom. For instance, a runny nose will get the cold out of your body and a fever will kill a virus. In his attempts to prove this hypothesis, he attempted to find a cure for Malaria which runs a high fever. To induce a high fever, he wanted to use arsenic but knew that arsenic is poisonous. He took real arsenic and diluted it, again and again. It is believed the remedy Arsenica contains the resonant energy of the original arsenic but has none of the negative properties. I have used these remedies on my son when he was little with great success. You can look up homeopathic remedies for stress relief and calm that are believed to activate the parasympathetic nervous system.

Resonate Exercises:

I. Aromatherapy:

This is the use of essential oils for calming or stimulating.

- Peppermint: Stimulating
- Orange: Focuses your attention
- Lavender: Calming
- Eucalyptus: Clearing

II. Colors: Use Color Psychology to change your mood

- Red and Pink: Related with love
- Blue: Calming and Happy
- Green: Vibrant
- White: Relieving

III. Use Crystals as an Energy Uplift

Many believe crystals contain energy. When you consider the years and conditions in nature needed to make them, it makes sense. Find a small-sized crystal to keep in your pocket. Use it as a talisman to remind you of your goals and to help cleanse your energy.

Here are some characteristics of common crystals, you can also wear them in jewelry:

- Amethyst: Stress Relief
- Quartz: Purification and Protection
- Turquoise: Connection to the earth
- Sapphire: Clearing/Spiritual Connection
- Ruby: Courage
- Moonstone: Protection, great for travel

Replenish Synonyms
Refill
Regenerate
Fill
Stock up
Reload
Increase
Augment

Replenish Antonyms:
Deplete
Reduce
Drain
Exhaust
Diminish
Run Down
Use up

STEP TEN: REPLENISH

"Every morning when I step into the shower, and the abundant, clean, hot water cascades over me, I can't help but give great thanks and feel true sense of gratitude, knowing not everyone has the same access to clean hot water." ~ Mary O'Leary Dronson

We all can take better care of ourselves. This step of the model is about staying positive and healthy. This is not always easy, so we need to find ways to **replenish** not only our body but our soul.

Years ago, I was stressed out about my job, and it began to show up as aches and pains in my body. While I began using chiropractic care, it helped my body, but it did not reduce my anxiety. I took a classical yoga class at a gym in Manayunk. It changed my life. I learned how to quiet my mind and take time to allow my thoughts to rest. I even continued my yoga practice on vacation. My friends thought I was weird when I did yoga in Avalon at the Jersey Shore. And on my trip to Hawaii, I did yoga on the beach every day to **replenish**. One day, a whale breached in front of me on Kaanapali Beach.

There are some remedies and body movements that can assist you in replenishing your body and sense of energy:

Hot Tea for Relaxation: Herbal teas such as Chamomile and other blends can help you rest and reset.

CALM: This is a magnesium-based product that can help you sleep at night

Meditation: This is simply learning how to focus on the present moment and remove the chatter from your thought patterns. Even one minute in the morning prepares you to remain calm throughout your day.

Rescue Remedy: This is an over-the-counter Bach flower essence made to calm you.

Techniques:

Calm Technique---Put one hand on your forehead and one hand on the base of your skull, and you will be pulled from the memory to the present

The Emotional Freedom Technique: This combines Chinese Acupressure with modern psychological approaches to recasting trauma memories. Tapping your left arm or thigh and then the right in a sequence triggers the parasympathetic calming response which reduces cortisol in the body and strengthens the immune system.

Metaphysics emphasizes the Law of Cause and Effect. What you put out to the universe in thought and speech returns multiplied at the same frequency. Finding out I am cause to my own effect was a bitter pill to swallow when I first began to study metaphysics. That is why replenishment is so important. You don't want to be giving out negative energy. You want to send out positivity and wear the shirt that says, Life is Good!

The Law of Circulation tells us that our possessions don't belong to us. Just like a baby bird must be released into the wild, try not to hold on to things so tightly. My mom used to tell the story about how my grandmother used to hold her parakeet Pixie so tightly, she would not come when called. My grandfather, on the other hand, would have Pixie sit on his shoulder, and she came to him every time he called.

Replenishment Story: The Tavistock Laboratory Course

In graduate school I enrolled in what turned out to be a difficult class called Tavistock. It was an intensive that met every day for ten days with a large group of 70 students. Unbeknownst to me, the program was designed specifically to create conflict. My friend Joe and I got in a massive fight in front of the whole group. The next day, we worked it out. When we went to the Week One closing session, the program coordinators criticized us. I replied, "There is no healing going on here." The coordinator said shockingly, "This is a laboratory, not a therapeutic environment." *Really?* I later learned that the course description proclaimed you should not take the class if you are in therapy. I completely disagree; you needed therapy to survive that class.

Joe noticed each day I returned to class, I was centered, happy and ready for a new challenge. He asked me, "What are you doing to handle the stress of this course?" To which I replied, "I am seeing my chiropractor, my therapist, and my acupuncturist, and I am using essential oils. Replenishment, calming the brain, is the best way out of stressful environments."

Replenishment Story: Master's Program at Temple and Group Dynamics Class at Ambler

During my master's study, I took a class at the Ambler campus of Temple University. This campus is where I first started at Temple in the suburbs and where I made all of my lifelong friends from college. Initially, I was thrilled to spend a week reliving the earlier days of my youth. How wrong I was! This was another class designed to bring out the worst in group dynamics. The class was so upsetting for me, I piled crystals into my pockets when I went to class to stave off the negative energy. I walked out of class one day because I was so stressed out over an argument about what someone said versus what she meant to say. I walked around the campus to refresh and take deep breaths to lower my level of anger. I walked outside to get some fresh air on the same campus where I first attended school as a freshman. I saw Cliff, the security guard, who had been there since that time. He looked at me and asked, "You are not going to let them get to you, are you?" *How did he know?*

It's amazing how a vote of support can lift one's spirits, and I knew immediately he was right. Bravely, I returned to the class to find that the other students in my class felt so guilty about how they argued with me, they were begging the instructor to give me an A even if I did not return. I returned to the class with my head held high and did receive an A. When I walked back into the class, they were discussing how to kill animals. It was bizarre. It was never about the animals; the group was using it as an analogy to subconsciously discuss what is actually going on in relationships. They tried to figuratively kill me and that's why they were having this macabre discussion. I learned a lot in the Psychoeducational Process program on how to deal with conflict and how to create learning and work environments that manage differing views and opinions safely to resolve conflict without anger and emotion.

Replenishment Story: The Two-Week Risk Control Tour

For a few years, I traveled to eight manufacturing facilities owned by my risk consulting client. Each time over a two-week period, I accompanied fire safety engineers on plant inspections. My job was to arrange the travel, schedule the right personnel, translate American English words to German or British English words. Every day, it was planes, trains, and automobiles. I enjoyed the way the trip suspended my life, yet it was stressful. To reduce my stress, I went out of my way to schedule hotels having lap swimming pools. My swim every morning replenished me, enhanced my mood, and set me in the right energy for the entire day, including whatever travel came after our tour. The men I traveled with were delightful, and we had a great time. I also scheduled a respite in Napa Valley between the two-week tour and met up with a good friend. The boys stayed in San Francisco and got to witness Fleet Week and the air acrobatics of Blue Angels, which I have seen many times.

Replenishment Exercises

I. Triggering the Parasympathetic Nervous System

- Go to an art museum.
- Visit a Frank Lloyd Wright-designed house.
- Do Pilates.
- Go swimming.
- Ride a bicycle.
- Walk the beach or a shoreline.
- Walk a labyrinth.
- Focus on your breath: Your breathing will be much deeper.
- Breathe like a baby pushing out your belly on the inhale.
- Get trained in a healing modality: Reiki, Touch for Health, Magnified Healing.
- Join a book club or study group.

- Hold an infant, a puppy, or a kitten.
- Go out and smell the flowers.
- Go birdwatching.
- Take time to meditate.
- Do something creative: write, draw, sing.
- Listen to soft, soothing music.
- Find a soothing environment.
- Get a massage.

Create a sanctuary space where you feel safe. t's good to define your safe space in advance.

II. Replenishment-How to activate your Parasympathetic Nervous System

Know yourself and your triggers.

Talk with a friend, counselor, or loved one.

Recognize and study your stress triggers.

Rehearse your stressful situations, such as delivering a speech, so you unlearn or override your fear.

Gather more information about your situation to dispel fear.

Engage in innovative techniques when communicating with others. Instead of saying "no," you can reply, "Yes, and ...." or "Can you elaborate?" The more information you have, the easier it will be to stay centered and connected.

III. Hydrate!

IN SUMMARY APPLYING THE CC MODEL
MY WORK WITH THE LABYRINTH—

THE LABYRINTH: CLARIFY—
MAKE A CHOICE

In 1993, I decided to take a corporate job which allowed me to attend a Holistic Health Training Program at Rosemont College. That one simple decision to turn down a high-powered job with an international insurance brokerage changed the trajectory of my life and career.

The intense program required six hours of class time and homework each week. We learned many alternative healing modalities. It was at the time when yoga and herbal tea were "weird." While in the program, I met my friend Suzanne McCall. She gave me an article on a meditative walking path known as a Labyrinth. I did not read the article, and I threw away the issue of New Age Magazine she had given me. Suzanne was also the person who introduced me and others to the teachings of Ernest Holmes.

THE LABYRINTH: CO-CREATE—
KNOW THAT YOU CAN MAKE THINGS HAPPEN

While on a business trip in San Francisco, my colleague and I took time to sightsee and asked me what I would like to do before our dinner plans. In that moment, I looked up and saw Grace Cathedral at the top of Knob Hill, and I announced, "I would like to go to that church." We found a parking spot on California and entered the magnificent cathedral. There I discovered the labyrinth! I didn't know the cathedral contained a labyrinth nor did I know anything about Veriditas which was founded to populate the world with labyrinths and use them in spiritual traditions. The Universe spoke very loudly, and the labyrinth found me. I had chills!

THE LABYRINTH: LETTING GO— RELEASE, TITHE, AND FORGIVE

After having such a profound experience through the labyrinth at Grace Cathedral, I donated $500 to the outdoor terrazzo labyrinth that was under construction at that time. I received a telephone call from Reverend Lauren Artress, the founder of Veriditas. She called to thank me for the large donation. During our call, I shared that I wanted to be trained as a Veriditas Labyrinth Facilitator, but I did not want to travel to San Francisco again. It turned out she was running an East Coast training only 45 minutes from my home in the suburbs of Philadelphia. I was able to commute to the training in Newark, DE. This training has brought amazing experiences into my life, and all because of my $500 contribution.

THE LABYRINTH: EMBODY— BRING YOUR DREAM INTO REALITY

It was after attending a Veriditas Retreat in the fall of 1999 in Racine, Wisconsin, that I was drawn by Rev. Lauren's call for the world to walk labyrinths as we entered the new millennium. Then, I called David Broida, the head of my township's Park and Recreation Department, and asked if he would allow me to run a walk for peace on New Year's Eve. He was more than happy to oblige, and we ran a beautiful event for almost 10 years at the Gulph Mills elementary school.

THE LABYRINTH: ENTERTAIN— THINK BIG

I really wanted to return to the CSL Asilomar conference and bring the labyrinth with me. My friend, Rev. Susan Sirutus connected me with Reverend

Jeffrey Proctor who was on the CSL conference committee. He welcomed the labyrinth, and every day I ran a workshop with the labyrinth and hosted an evening of walking it with music. It was incredibly profound and I learned from all the great ministerial teachers of the spiritual doctrine, all of whom have been kind enough to give us quotes. For over ten years, I spent a week on the Pacific Ocean learning and teaching in a special bubble that we rarely find in this busy life. I think back fondly of using the pay phone to check my work voicemail. It was before cell phones and email when it was much easier to take a real break. I thank Rev. Jeffrey Proctor for the amazing experience which is now woven into the fabric of my life. Jeffrey passed away too early but the memory of his generosity of spirit lingers on.

THE LABYRINTH: AFFIRM— BOLDLY TELL SPIRIT WHAT YOU ARE SEEKING

As previously told, I met my husband Ron, within an hour of declaring that I was seeking a partner at the Grace Cathedral/Veriditas Labyrinth facilitator reunion.

THE LABYRINTH: ATTEND— PAY ATTENTION TO YOUR ACTIONS AND YOUR GUIDANCE AND YOUR DESIRES

Years before the labyrinth and 9/11, I purchased tickets to the 1996 Olympics. I planned to attend with my friend Suzanne who introduced me to the labyrinth and my good friend from college Ruth Lynch and her husband, Fred. Suzanne called me after we acquired the tickets and told me that she was conflicted. She wanted to attend a one week or one month seminar in San Francisco at the California Institute for Integral Studies; it was a course on Expressive Arts Therapy. A week or so later I experienced an incredibly vivid dream that the four of us were in a staging area in Germany to go into war-torn Bosnia as humanitarian aids. We could not decide if we should go for one week or one month. Intuitively, I knew the dream was guiding me to join Suzanne in San Francisco. I called Ruth and she happily announced she was pregnant and would be fine cancelling our trip. We gave the tickets to friends, and I called Suzanne and let her know we were going to CIIS for the class. The class was remarkable. We studied the healing power of the mind known as psychoimmunology, art therapy, and a form of spiritual psychology known as Psychosynthesis. It was an incredibly healing week. We went to Los Angeles first and imagine my shock to see the bombing at the Atlanta Olympics. I had two friends who were very close to the event, and it was a miracle that the bomb did not operate as planned. We then flew to San Francisco, and it was on that journey that Suzanne introduced me to David Monks, who went to High School with Ron. Because I traveled to San Francisco so frequently, we kept in touch and became close friends.

THE LABYRINTH: RESONATE— SEND OUT POSITIVE ENERGY TO CHANGE THE WORLD AND SUPPORT YOURSELF

The labyrinth comes from many different indigenous traditions around the world. The different labyrinths are Jungian archetypes. It's believed that the ancient labyrinth patterns transcend time and space, and we all walk together as we walk a centuries old pattern. My work running labyrinth walks has led me to provide transformative experiences to over 2,000 labyrinth walkers. This volunteer work has served to enhance my psychic abilities, my introspection, my acceptance and my personal transformation. Giving to others through my labyrinth work has returned to me in kind over and over again.

THE LABYRINTH: REPLENISH— TAKE TIME TO NOURISH YOUR MIND, BODY, AND SOUL

The purpose of walking a labyrinth is to take time to reflect, release, and renew. The more you can connect with your thoughts, desires, and concerns and sort all of that out, the better you are at succeeding on this earth. **Replenishment** can come from nature, the labyrinth, forgiveness, breathing, yoga, exercise, or anything that brings you joy, even the laughter of a small child.

IN SUMMARY:

You can take charge of what happens in your life. Set your intentions, do the hard cleansing work and find ways to retrain your brain to be calmer with less anxiety. That is when great things happen!

RESOURCES

Website Links to Research that support Ten Steps of the Clarity Concepts ™ Coaching Model

Clarify: Research on Goal Setting by Leslie Riopel, MSc.

- https://positivepsychology.com/benefits-goal-setting

Co-Creation: Research on the Psychoneuroimmunology and the Placebo Effect by Dr. Lissa Rankin and Dr. Kaptchuk

- https://lissarankinmd.com/p/mind-over-medicine-6-steps
- https:health.harvard.edu/mental-health/the-power-of-the-placebo-effect

Love: Research on Gratitude by Researcher Chih-Che Lin, Dr. Asif Amin, Joshua Brown, and Joel Wong

- https://positivepsychology.com/benefits-gratitude-research-questions/
- http:greatergood.berkley.edu/article/item/how_gratitude_changes_you_and_ your_brain

Letting Go: Forgiveness Research by Dr. Fred Luskin of the Stanford Forgiveness Project

- http://greatergood.berkley.edu/topic/forgiveness
- https://greatergood.berkeley.edu/article/item/fred_luskin_explains_how_to_forgive

Embody: Research on Exercise and Visualization for Sports Performance by Dr. Tim Barclay and Elizabeth Quinn, MS

- https://www.innerbody.com/mental-health-benefits-of-exercise
- https://www.verywellfit.com/visualization-techniques-for-athletes-3119438

Entertain: Research on Casting a wide net to make better decisions by The Chip and Dean Heath

- https://heathbrothers.com/books/decisive/

Attend: Research on Mindfulness by Dr. Jeremy Sutton

- https://www.calminggrace.com/mindfulness-pay-attention
- What Is Mindfulness? Definition, Benefits & Psychology (positivepsychology.com)

Resonate: Research on Happiness by Drs. Grant & Glueck and Laughter Dr. Matthew Miller

- www.forbes.com/sites/georgebradt/2015/05/27/the-secret-of-happiness-revealed-by-harvard-study/?sh=135013f0e6786
- The Science of Laughter (wanderlust.com)

Replenish: Benefits of Meditation studies at Harvard, Emory, and Heart Math Institute

- www.health.harvard.edu/staying-healthy/what-meditation-can-do-for-your-mind-...
- https://www.heartmath.org/
- Mind Over Matters | Emory University | Atlanta GA

DEDICATIONS:

Thank you to my mother, Helen Noyes Downey, who taught me how to read and write. A special thank you to my Honors English teachers at Abington High School (PA) who taught me how to organize my thoughts with impact: Mr. Winters, Mrs. Stern, Ms. Foley, and Mrs. Tobin.

Thank you to all of the holistic healers with whom I have studied: Elsie Kerns (Reiki), Lorraine DiGiovanni, Dr. Lili Mansi (Reiki), The Rosemont Sisters of the Holy Child, Rosemont College & The Medical Mission Sisters in the Health Perspectives Certificate program, Chris Aldworth (Magnified Healing) and Dr. Lauren Artress at the Veriditas Labyrinth Institute, formerly at Grace Cathedral.

Thank you to those with whom I learned and studied Psychology, including Dr. Thomas Legere & Rev. Paula Legere, Dr. Cheri Franklin, The California Institute for Integral Studies and The Psychoeducational Processes (PEP) program at Temple University's School of Education.

Thank you to the many corporate soft skills training programs in which I learned Public Speaking techniques, Selling Skills, Negotiations skills Personality Profiles and Differences, Neuro Linguistic Programming and Emotional Intelligence. Thank you to my education at the Temple University Fox School of Business which lead me into my Risk Management career and entrepreneurship.

Thank you to the teachers that I was fortunate to learn from at my Center for Spiritual Living/Science of Mind Center (CSL Philly) including Rev. Gwen Gillespie, Rev. Susan Sirutus, Dr. Bob Deen, Rev. Mike Gerdes, and Dr. Maxine Kaye.

Thank you to the Greats in the CSL teaching whose Asilomar and Center talks have inspired me for the 30 years I have been expanding and growing in God-awareness through the CSL teaching including: Dr. James Mellon, Rev. Dr. David Ault, Dr. Karen Drucker, Dr. David Walker, Dr. Tom Costa, Dr. Stuart Grayson, Dr. Jay Scott Neale, Dr. Edward Viljoen, Dr. Joe Hooper, Dr. David Leonard, Dr. Kenn Gordon, Dr. Dennis Merritt Jones, Dr. Arleen Bump, and Dr. Jim Lockhard.

Thank you to Dr. Kennedy Shultz whose talk at the induction of CSL Philly inspired me to live and breathe the CSL teaching of Ernest Holmes. Many thanks to Rev. Dr. Jeffrey Proctor, may he rest in peace, who trusted me with the incredible opportunity to work at the annual CSL conference creating labyrinth walks, workshops, and music nights for ten years by the sea at Asilomar State Conference Grounds in Pacific Grove, CA. The experiences were life-altering.

Finally, thank you to the Power of 8 Circle from The Spiritual Center of the Desert (Palm Desert) lead by Rev. Gail Morton and joined with Religious Science Practitioners Lesia Kohut and Aimee Shapiro. I don't think I would have had such a healthy and successful 2022 without their support, intention, and vision. Thank you to my patient editor Claudia Volkman and to my copy editor Dr. Maureen Hoyt.

Lastly, I thank my son Mackie DenBroeder, who has made this journey so worthwhile.

GLOSSARY

Cause and Effect: The law that what you put out is returned to you; Love will bring you Love, Hate will bring you Hate

Consciousness: Being aware of this very moment and your though patterns

Co-Create: Your innate ability to work with spirit to create your desired outcomes

Demonstration: The Results that appear in your life as the result of your intentional co-creation

New Thought: Phineas P. Quimby is widely recognized as the founder of the New Thought movement. Born in Lebanon, New Hampshire but raised in Belfast, Maine, Quimby learned about the power of the mind to heal through hypnosis.

Mental Equivalent: The Principle that thought Patterns create the outcomes in your life. Some of these thought patterns are subconscious and unknown to us. We can look at our life outcomes to uncover these.

Law of Attraction: The Principle that *Like attracts Like*; if you are filled with positive energy, positive things will occur. If something negative occurs, work diligently to find the positive in the experience to prevent further negativity.

Manifest: To make something happen on the physical plane; to see a result from your actions and thoughts and intentional prayer; a manifestation is the thing you helped create.

Treatment: Affirmative prayer. A method of working with spirit to communicate what it is you desire; a process of knowing your desired outcome will present itself. This can be done in a single command if you truly believe the outcome is possible. It also requires letting go of anything in the way of your outcome.

Law of Circulation: The concept that in giving you will receive. Sharing is caring. This is the biblical tenet of tithing or in modern day vernacular, "*Pay it Forward*". Its based on the concept that nothing belongs to you. Your job is to live in the flow of abundance.

Tithe: Giving to those who serve and support you. Biblical concept that you will experience abundance if you share a % of your income with your church or spiritual center or those that serve your growth and progress.

Abundance: Having plenty. Abundance includes financial prosperity, but it also includes abundance of friendship, support, love, beauty, adventure, health, family, etc. The list is endless.

Synchronicity: Coincidental occurrence of events; this is more likely to occur when we have an awareness of our surroundings-look for the familiar. With social media, its much easier to connect with friends and family in unexpected places.

ABOUT THE AUTHOR

Jane Marie Downey, M. Ed grew up in Meadowbrook, Pennsylvania. Jane is the oldest of five children.

After graduating from Abington High School, Jane took a gap year and opened Hechinger's, the big box home improvement center in Jenkintown. Walking into an empty store with 100 people was an amazing business and group dynamics education. From there, she entered business school at Temple University's Fox school of business where she became fascinated with Risk Management because it involved so many modalities: insurance, finance, legal, language, engineering and much more. She has become an internationally known insurance and risk management expert and educator and often gives testimony in litigation concerning insurance disputes. When Jane started her risk consulting practice, she was able to obtain a master's degree from Temple in Psychoeducational processes, the study of group behavior, which enabled her to add Leadership Development to her consulting practice.

Early in her career, when Jane returned to the Philadelphia area after working in New York for five years, she made a choice, which she shares in the book, to take a position that allowed her to study holistic health.

She was the oddball at her group shore house in Avalon, NJ when she did yoga on the deck in the early 90's. Jane has been working with her Clarity Concepts coaching model now for 26 years. Some time ago, she realized she had to share her life stories to convince her readers that her plan works. Now, long after the model came to Jane in a meditation, all of the ten steps have been verified and grounded in research. No longer is meditation weird or herbal remedies outliers. We are all now working with integrative models to create positive living,

www.ingramcontent.com/pod-product-compliance
Lightning Source LLC
Chambersburg PA
CBHW031419120626
46545CB00006B/2175